"I have experienced in the past the storms of unexpected serious illness. Marc Maillefer speaks biblically and from close personal experience into this situation. This is a wonderful book which I warmly recommend. Take its helpful medicine and it will calm many a storm!"

>   RT. REVD. WALLACE BENN, Bishop of Lewes, and
>   President of Church of England Evangelical Council

"The thoughts and stories in this truly pastoral book give fresh lustre to the precious truth that our God is indeed with his people in trouble."

>   J. I. PACKER, Professor of Theology,
>   Regent College

"I was helped personally by a fresh realization that God has a purpose for the storms in our lives. I have taken the liberty of passing along the manuscript to a friend in the midst of a storm."

>   KENNETH N. TAYLOR, Chairman of the Board,
>   Tyndale House

"*God in the Storm* offers a secure lifeline when unexpected waves overwhelm us. Here is a book we can trust. It comes from an author who has known rough waters and assures us that God's Word is strong enough to navigate the course home."

>   DAVID HELM, Senior Pastor,
>   Holy Trinity Church, Chicago

"Marc Maillefer writes from deeply personal and pastoral experience, informed by the Scripture's strong and comforting truths about God's sovereign purpose and care for his people. In his words and life, Marc has encouraged me with his living example of God's gracious provision in the storms."

>   NIEL NIELSON, President, Covenant College,
>   former pastoral colleague, College Church in Wheaton, Illinois

GOD IN THE STORM

MARC MAILLEFER

CROSSWAY BOOKS

A MINISTRY OF
GOOD NEWS PUBLISHERS
WHEATON, ILLINOIS

God in the Storm

Copyright © 2005 by Marc Maillefer

Published by Crossway Books
        A ministry of Good News Publishers
        1300 Crescent Street
        Wheaton, Illinois 60187

Cover design: Josh Dennis

Cover photo: Photonica

First printing, 2005

Printed in the United States of America

Unless otherwise indicated, all Scripture quotations are taken from the *English Standard Version*®. Copyright © 2001 by Crossway Bibles, a division of Good News Publishers. Used by permission.

Scriptures indicated as from NLT are taken from *New Living Translation*, copyright © 1996 by Tyndale Charitable Trust. Used by permission.

Library of Congress Cataloging-in-Publication Data
Maillefer, Marc A.
  God in the storm / Marc Maillefer.
    p. cm.
  ISBN 1-58134-648-4 (tpb)
    1. Suffering—Biblical teaching. 2. Suffering—Religious aspects—
Christianity. 3. Bible—Criticism, interpretation, etc. I. Title.
BS680.S854M25   2004
248.8'6—dc22   2004020108

CH		14	13	12	11	10	09	08	07	06	05
15	14	13	12	11	10	9	8	7	6	5	4	3	2	1

To Lori,

*For your grace and strength in the storm and
for the joys you have brought to me —
Laura, Bridget, Claire, Peter, and Luke.
Your love and companionship are my delight.*

CONTENTS

FOREWORD

By R. Kent Hughes

Marc Maillefer is a happy man who sings and whistles his way through the day. I know because I often hear him through the double doors of my office! And he moves fast, descending the stairs at the speed of a drumroll. He's a can-do, go-to man who can keep several balls in the air.

Marc is a lover of people and a devoted family man. His lovely wife, Lori, is known for her hospitality, and as a result the Maillefer home is full not only with their five children but with a flood of guests from the church and their neighborhood. And all of this is what makes *God in the Storm* so real and captivating — it was written when the storm of Lori's bout with cancer was not over, amidst the busy, buoyant life I have just described.

To be sure there were many dark days and tears and abiding uncertainties, but there has always been an outwardness and other-directedness to the Maillefers' lives.

It is this positive authenticity, plus the utter biblicalness of what Pastor Maillefer writes, plus the wide-ranging testimonials from other sufferers that gives this book such power.

Most of all this book is about God — the God of the storms — God with us — God's purpose for the storms — the God who provides — God's grace in the storms.

This book will set the suffering soul free to sing about God.

PREFACE

God does good things through the hard times of life. Two years ago my wife, the mother of our five children, was diagnosed with breast cancer. My desire in writing this book is to help you understand that godly people, like Job, can and will suffer. My prayer is that God would be glorified through the suffering in your life as you worship him through tears, submitting to his good purposes, blessing his name. All this demonstrates to a watching world that Jesus Christ is far better than anything the world can give. He is better than our health, riches, and dare I say family.

I am sure that the only way our experience and these words will help is if they are connected to God's Word. May this book draw you to Christ, the living Word, and make you more like him.

Soli Deo Gloria.

ACKNOWLEDGMENTS

Special thanks to my loving family who stood with us in the storm. I also want to thank our family at College Church for the way in which they tangibly shared the love of Christ with us. Thanks to my friends who contributed words of wisdom (included in the appendix). I am indebted to Lane Dennis for hearing these sermons and thinking they could help others and for Ted Griffin who smoothed out the rough edges. Thanks also to Kent Hughes, my pastor, mentor, and friend for over twenty-one years.

There was a man in the land of Uz whose name was Job, and that man was blameless and upright, one who feared God and turned away from evil. There were born to him seven sons and three daughters. He possessed 7,000 sheep, 3,000 camels, 500 yoke of oxen, and 500 female donkeys, and very many servants, so that this man was the greatest of all the people of the east. His sons used to go and hold a feast in the house of each one on his day, and they would send and invite their three sisters to eat and drink with them. And when the days of the feast had run their course, Job would send and consecrate them, and he would rise early in the morning and offer burnt offerings according to the number of them all. For Job said, "It may be that my children have sinned, and cursed God in their hearts." Thus Job did continually.

Now there was a day when the sons of God came to present themselves before the LORD, *and Satan also came among them. The* LORD *said to Satan, "From where have you come?" Satan answered the* LORD *and said, "From going to and fro on the earth, and from walking up and down on it." And the* LORD *said to Satan, "Have you considered my servant Job, that there is none like him on the earth, a blameless and upright man, who fears God and turns away from evil?" Then Satan answered the* LORD *and said, "Does Job fear God for no reason? Have you not put a hedge around him and his house and all that he has, on every side? You have blessed the work of his hands, and his possessions have increased in the land. But stretch out your hand and touch all that he has, and he will curse you to your face." And the* LORD *said to Satan, "Behold, all that he has is in your hand. Only against him do not stretch out your hand." So Satan went out from the presence of the* LORD.*

Now there was a day when his sons and daughters were eating and drinking wine in their oldest brother's house, and there came a messenger to Job and said, "The oxen were plowing and the donkeys feeding beside them, and the Sabeans fell upon them and took them and struck down the servants with the edge of the sword, and I alone have escaped to tell you." While he was yet speaking, there came another and said, "The fire of God fell from heaven and burned up the sheep and the servants and consumed them, and I alone have escaped to tell you." While he was yet speaking, there came another and said, "The Chaldeans formed three groups and made a raid on the camels and took them and struck down the servants with the edge of the sword, and I alone have escaped to tell you." While he was yet speaking, there came another and said, "Your sons and daughters were eating and drinking wine in their oldest brother's house, and behold, a great wind came across the wilderness and struck the four corners of the house, and it fell upon the young people, and they are dead, and I alone have escaped to tell you."

Then Job arose and tore his robe and shaved his head and fell on the ground and worshiped. And he said, "Naked I came from my mother's womb, and naked shall I return. The LORD gave, and the LORD has taken away; blessed be the name of the LORD."

In all this Job did not sin or charge God with wrong.

JOB 1:1-22, ESV

1

GOD OF
THE STORMS

In a single week in Chicago, a porch collapsed in Lincoln Park leaving eighteen dead, and another porch in that great city became the target of a car careening out of control, killing five young children. Two high school graduates died just down the road when their car hit a tree. In my own life at that time, my friend Willis Jones breathed his last.

Storms do come. Are we ready for them? How should we think about such times of affliction — about God's role in them, and our response to them? How do you make sense of life when you are in the midst of an especially difficult trial? In the following pages we will explore God's role over the storms, his presence in them, his purposes for the storms, his provisions in the storm, and finally his grace through the storms.

Job was a man whose whole world was devastated by such storms. The beauty of this book of the Bible is that it tells us as much about God and his sovereignty as it does about Job's suffering. Unlike the storms we go through, the book of Job gives us the behind-the-scenes look. We see what Job never saw and what we don't see in our own trials. We know things about Job's story that he never knew. We see the "wager" drafted in the throne room of heaven when God presented Job as his righteous man. We see how it all ends as well. Job never had the information given to us in the prologue (chapters 1 — 2). Job didn't have a clue how it would end; chapter 42 had yet to be written.

Job's experience is like ours. The storms cloud our vision, leaving us groping for answers. *Why is this happening? Who is responsible? When will it end? Why me?*

The biblical account gives a much-needed perspective on our suffering. We are reminded that not all suffering is linked to our sin. We learn that God sometimes brings calamity even to his righteous followers. We learn that those who try to get God "off the hook" so to speak end up misrepresenting God and needing his forgiveness.

But lest we expect that the advantage we are given in seeing Job's storm from the end to the beginning will remove all our questions, we must remind ourselves up front that God's Word, with its truth about suffering and sovereignty, will not tell us everything we want to know. Questions are dealt with, but the fact is, mystery remains.

A quick review of Job 1 makes it clear that Job is a righteous man (vv. 1-5), our God is a sovereign God (vv. 6-12), even the righteous will suffer (vv. 13-19) and finally, even in suffering we can worship God (vv. 20-22).

THE RIGHTEOUSNESS OF JOB

The chapter begins by telling us that Job was "blameless," "upright," a God-fearer, and one who "turned away from evil." This fourfold description of righteous Job is repeated by God again (v. 8), making it clear to all of us that Job was more than a good man. He was a righteous man who lived a godly life.

Job's godly character was matched by his wealth (God does not always reward his faithful followers in this way — it is his sovereign choice). The first sign of his wealth was his ten children — seven sons and three daughters. In addition to that, he had seven thousand sheep, three thousand camels, five hundred yoke of oxen, and five hundred female donkeys. Verse 3 ends with the phrase, "this man was the greatest of all the people of the east"— greatest in his position, greatest in his possessions, greatest in his righteousness toward God and others.

His righteous character is even more amazing when we understand that in the face of great prosperity he did not succumb to self-sufficiency, to an attitude that says, "I don't need you, God." He was a righteous man who knew God and feared God. He understood who God was and responded accordingly. His relationship with God was marked by a reverent, affectionate, humble obedience.

Not only that, but verses 4-5 tell us that righteous Job was concerned for his whole family. Like a priest he offered sacrifices for his children, just in case they had sinned and cursed God, and we are told this was Job's regular practice. Job was a righteous man.

THE SOVEREIGNTY OF GOD

As the text moves from Job to God, it also takes us from earth up to heaven. We see here that God is King over everything and everyone. Even Satan needs God's permission to test his theory (vv. 9-11). Satan was convinced that the only reason Job worshiped God was because God had blessed him and put a hedge around him.

> *"Does Job fear God for no reason? Have you not put a hedge around him and his house and all that he has, on every side? You have blessed the work of his hands, and his possessions have increased in the land. But stretch out your hand and touch all that he has, and he will curse you to your face."*

Satan concluded that Job's prosperity came from God. That was true. God was sovereign over Job's life and possessions. But Satan was wrong in thinking that Job (or any follower of God) would only worship him during good times. "Take away the good times, the good things, and he will curse you to your face." That is what Satan thought; so he asked God to stretch out his hand and touch all that Job had.

> And the LORD said to Satan, "Behold, all that he has is in your hand. Only against him do not stretch out your hand." So Satan went out from the presence of the LORD. (v. 12)

God is sovereign — he is King over all things, in heaven above and here on earth. He not only allowed Satan to "touch" Job (2:5-6), but in 2:3b God said something to Satan that is shocking: "you incited me against him to destroy him without reason."

The shocking thing here is the proximity of our good and perfect God to the evil and trials that Job suffered. The same juxtaposition shows up in the life of Joseph. Joseph says to his brothers, "you meant evil against me, but God meant it for good, to bring it about that many people should be kept alive" (Genesis 50:20). This is the verse that Lisa Beamer (the widow of Todd Beamer, killed on 9/11 by terrorists) often writes under her signature. Behind the wicked scheming of his scoundrel brothers, Joseph saw a sovereign God who is good — and so must we! More on this point later.

JOB'S STORM

I remember well the night my family was camping at Peninsula State Park in northern Wisconsin. My wife Lori and I had our tent, the boys had another, and the girls a third (why did it take us so long to figure out the beauty of multiple tents?). I woke up in the middle of the night to the sound of distant thunder, echoing over the waters of Green Bay. Lori and I were both awake and wondered how soon it would roll through our campsite. Would the storm last long? Would it be one of those storms that has you packing it all in, in the middle of the night? The booming thunder was ominous, but it was still a ways off, leaving us plenty of time to prepare. And prepare we did. I ran through our campsite tossing things into the car. I woke the kids and told them to move their sleeping bags and anything else off the edges. We were ready for the storm!

But often that is not how the storms of life work. Most storms leave us no time to prepare. I think of two phone calls that rocked my world. The first came on Wednesday morning, December 11, 2002. I was preparing a message in my study at home when Dr. Hawkins called — I assumed to give the results of my wife's mammogram. "Hello. Maillefers. Marc speaking." "Yes, this is Dr. Hawkins. Is Lori there?" "No, she's out for a bit — do you have any information on her mammogram?" "Just have her call me." In that moment I was sure that Lori had breast cancer.

I wasn't ready for this storm, and a paralyzing fear was driven deep into my heart. The dread was suffocating, and it all happened in a moment. For the next hour I sat in my chair gripped with fear, wondering how it was all going to play out. There was no warning. Lightning struck out of a clear blue sky.

The second call came on May 9, 2003. It was Lori, and she asked me if I had heard. Her trembling voice let me know that the news I was about to hear was not good. She told me she had just checked the messages on our phone and that my dad had called to say that my healthy mom had died that morning. Once again there was no warning, no time to prepare. To be sure not every storm begins with a violent lightning strike. Some roll in slowly, like that storm over the lake. But storms often catch us completely by surprise. I have long used the phrase, "You never know what a day will hold." Little did I know how true that is until my own storms came.

Job was not prepared for the four servants who staggered in with tragic news. Everything he had — from his oxen to his sheep, from his servants to his ten children and their families — had been destroyed. One after the other, Job's servants pummeled him with the news, like a series of tidal waves, each one bigger than the next, and each sufficient to put him under. Job later said, speaking of God, "you toss me about in the roar of the storm" (Job 30:22).

The story of Job teaches us that as God's followers we should be prepared to suffer. Those who love him, who even live exemplary lives by his grace, are not exempt from the storms. Righteous, innocent Job suffered. Does your theology have room for suffering, or do you think Satan's right — that God lets us live in little bubbles to hedge us in from all pain, experiencing only blessing? Jesus said, "In the world you will have tribulation" (John 16:33). Paul said it as well in Acts 14:22: "Through many tribulations we must enter the kingdom of God." James says, "Count it all joy, my brothers, when [not if] you meet trials of various kinds" (James 1:2,).

Job himself understood that suffering was a possibility for a righteous God-fearer like himself. In Job 3:25 he said that the thing he feared and dreaded had come to pass — I assume he meant the loss of his children.

The interesting thing about the book of Job is that chapters 4 — 31 contain the speeches of Job's three "friends" who didn't believe that the righteous suffer innocently. They were convinced and tried to convince Job that the reason he was in that storm was because of sin somewhere in his life.

> Remember: who that was innocent ever perished? Or where were the upright cut off? As I have seen, those who plow iniquity and sow trouble reap the same. By the breath of God they perish, and by the blast of his anger they are consumed. (Job 4:7-9)

Suffering because of our transgressions is definitely a possibility. Ever since Adam and Eve disobeyed God, we have each suffered the consequences of sin — theirs and our own. But Job reminds us that within God's sovereign purposes the righteous may suffer innocently.

SUFFERERS WHO WORSHIP

Our worship to God suffers when sufferers don't worship. Have you met a suffering worshiper? If you have, you have been encouraged. It happened again to me on a recent high school mission trip to Chicago. What a beautiful thing to see Karen Chong, a high school senior, stand before thirty senior adults testifying about God's grace in her father's life and in her family's life. A few months earlier, Karen's dad had died of pancreatic cancer after a short six-month battle. She shared the hope of the gospel with these new friends, many of whom were approaching the valley of the shadow of death. For over twenty minutes Karen eloquently and powerfully shared her testimony. I was completely taken aback by this young woman's faith. She sent me a follow-up letter that ended with these words:

> "As the heavens are higher than the earth, so are my ways higher than your ways and my thoughts than your thoughts." Isa 55:9 Although I don't know why my dad was taken from me, I do know that I can trust in his [God's] will and plan. This past week has confirmed that even more. Because he works for his glory, I desire God's will more than to have my dad here with me. This trip really served to reaffirm my faith, to encourage my heart, to reveal what it means to worship through grief, and to give me a greater burden for the lost.

How do we worship in the midst of suffering?

> *Then Job arose and tore his robe and shaved his head and fell on the ground and worshiped. And he said, "Naked I came from my mother's womb, and naked shall I return. The LORD gave, and the LORD has taken away; blessed be the name of the LORD."* (1:20-21)

Notice three things about Job's worship. First, he fell before God weeping and mourning over his great loss. Everything he felt, all the pain, all his tears, all the heartache — he brought it all to God.

Second, he submitted to God, acknowledging that he was nothing and God was everything. He said in essence, "I came into this world with nothing, and I am leaving with nothing." He acknowledged that all he had was from God. All he had belonged to God, and God had the right to take it away. Job submitted and worshiped by surrendering to God's sovereignty over every inch of his life — over every precious possession, even his ten beloved children.

Third, he blessed God. Although tempted to put God on trial, Job chose to praise God for his holy character and to bless his name. Throughout the book we find Job asking for an audience with God: "Give me a mediator to talk to you, God" (see 9:33; 31:35). Unable to put the pieces together, Job longed to hear from God; he longed for God to explain it all to him. But God was silent (but be sure of this — Job's feelings weren't). Job didn't respond on the basis of how he felt. Rather, from the depths of his heart he blessed God for who he was, even when his pain blurred his view of the character of God. And in so doing Job did not sin — he did not charge God with wrongdoing (1:21).

Are you in a storm today? Then fall before God weeping and mourning — he will not cast you out. This is part of your worship, to bring your brokenness to him. "The LORD is near to the brokenhearted" (Psalm 34:18). Many sufferers are overwhelmed at how strong their emotions are when they come to church. After Lori's first surgery (lumpectomy), I went to church and slipped into a side gallery, hoping no one would notice me. My heart was breaking. We had just heard that the surgeon did not get clear margins and that the cancer had spread to two lymph nodes. The opening hymn began, but I couldn't sing. All I could do was cry. My heart was aching so deeply, all that would come out was groans and tears. I had heard many say, "Pastor, it's too hard to go to church." I had never understood before, but I did then.

We cry, we ache, we feel embarrassed or overwhelmed at our inability to keep our emotions in check, and mistakenly we conclude, "I can't go back to church until I get it together." No, a thousand times no! We go to church to get put back together. Jesus said, "Come to me, all who are weary and heavy laden, and I will give you rest." Stay with God's people in your suffering — you need them, and they need you. Pour out your broken heart in worship! Allow your brothers and sisters in Christ to share the burden that will crush you if you carry it alone.

Are you in a storm today? Then fall on your face and acknowledge God as sovereign King. You may not be able to put it all together. I can't either. The great minds of the faith can't tie up every loose thread. There is much mystery.

James 5:11 gives us the "CliffsNotes" on the book of Job.

> *Behold, we consider those blessed who remained steadfast. You have heard of the steadfastness of Job, and you have seen the purpose of the Lord, how the Lord is compassionate and merciful.*

James is telling us that the book of Job is not just about Job's steadfast faith; it is about God's sovereignty, which is always accompanied by his compassion and mercy. Everything that happened to Job, including the most difficult and painful circumstances, was part of God's sovereign, loving plan. So when the book ends (42:11) we read from the pen of the author, not one of his misguided friends, these words:

> *Then came to him all his brothers and sisters and all who had known him before, and ate bread with him in his house. And they showed him sympathy and comforted him for all the evil that the LORD had brought upon him.*

Isaiah 45:7 says, "I form light and create darkness, I make wellbeing and bring calamity, I am the LORD, who does all these things." The Lord is all-powerful and always good. He tempts no one. He is just, and his character is pure — he is altogether holy. As sovereign he reigns over all things, and all things that come to us come from him. Even suffering and pain come from him. This is the conclusion of Job, his wife, his family, the author of the book of Job, Satan, and God himself (see 2:3). This picture of God shakes us to the core. What we do with this mysterious doctrine is critical. Some will play man's free choice against God's sovereignty. Others will set God's goodness against his power, as did Rabbi Harold Kushner, who in a recent interview said:

> For my part, if I must choose between an all-powerful God who is not kind and fair, who could have prevented the Holocaust or the birth of the deformed child and chose not to, or else a kind and fair God who is awesomely powerful but not omnipotent, I choose to affirm God's goodness even at the expense of his power.[1]

On the other side is Lisa Beamer, whose husband Todd was tragically killed on United Airlines Flight 93 on September 11, 2001 in the fields of Pennsylvania. She writes, "He [God] knew my children would be left without a father and me without a husband. Yet in his sovereignty and in his perspective on the big picture, he knew it was better to allow the events to unfold as they did rather than redirect Todd's plans to avoid death. I can't see all the reasons he might have allowed this when I know he could have stopped it. . . . I don't like how his plan looks from my perspective right now, but knowing that he loves me and can see the world from start to finish helps me say, 'It's OK.'"[2]

Dr. Mark Talbot recently spoke on this very thing to the students at Wheaton College as he talked about his injury thirty-five years ago that left him profoundly disabled. From the beginning he was convinced that nothing good and nothing bad happens to us that does not ultimately come from God's hand. He says, "Yet my accident's enduring effect has been that although I doubted God's existence before it happened, ever since, my physical condition has assured me that God loves me, especially when new physiological complications arise."[3]

The implications regarding God's character and free choice are huge — too big to get into in a few short pages. The mystery cannot, should not be removed, lest like Job's three friends we say things that we will need to repent of because we tried to get God "off the hook." There is no wickedness or evil in him even though he ordains the storms of life. Submit to his rule in your life, and trust his goodness.

Early in my family's storm I concluded: God is sovereign, and God is good. As severe as it is, Lori's cancer is God's good hand in our life. I want to say to my five children, now ages six to eighteen, that no matter what happens, God means to use it for good. Believing this was God's loving hand in our life we began to look for God's goodness. I started a journal, and for the better part of four months I kept a record of God's favor toward us. There was never a day when I didn't have something to write. Bless the Lord for who he is and what he is doing.

Job's wife said, "Curse God and die" (2:9). In other words, "Get it over with, Job. Do yourself and all of us a favor." But instead Job blessed the name of the Lord and did not sin with his mouth or charge God with wrong. Many today, as they reflect on suffering and go through painful trials, sin with their mouths. Let us not throw God's sovereignty overboard. In the introduction to his book *The Misery of Job and the Mercy of God*, John Piper writes: "The very thing the tilting ship needs in the storm is the ballast of God's good sovereignty, not the unburdening of deep and precious truth. What makes the crush of calamity sufferable is not that God shares our shock, but that his bitter providences are laden with the bounty of love."[4]

Looking at the cross we will see this even more clearly. Jesus was delivered up "according to the definite plan and foreknowledge of God" (Acts 2:23). Herod and Pontius Pilate did whatever God had predestined to take place (Acts 4:28); yet they did it of their free accord. They, along with the Jews, were guilty of his blood, and so are we. God used Christ's death and resurrection as the two greatest events in all of history. If God ordained the cross for his only Son, is it possible that he ordained the storm you are in? Of course it is. And if God could accomplish his best when mankind did their worst, do you believe he can bring good out of your trials? Of course he can. God is still looking for sufferers who worship him. May God help us to bless his name at all times through all the storms of life.

> *Oh, the depth of the riches and wisdom and knowledge of God! How unsearchable are his judgments and how inscrutable his ways! "For who has known the mind of the Lord, or who has been his counselor?" "Or who has given a gift to him that he might be repaid?" For from him and through him and to him are all things. To him be glory forever. Amen. (Romans 11:33-36)*

SCRIPTURES FOR REFLECTION

> *Arise, O LORD; O God, lift up your hand; forget not the afflicted. . . . O LORD, you hear the desire of the afflicted; you will strengthen their heart; you will incline your ear.* (PSALM 10:12, 17)

> *Behold, I have refined you, but not as silver; I have tried you in the furnace of affliction.* (ISAIAH 48:10)

> *But we have this treasure in jars of clay, to show that the surpassing power belongs to God and not to us. We are afflicted in every way, but not crushed; perplexed, but not driven to despair; persecuted, but not forsaken; struck down, but not destroyed; always carrying in the body the death of Jesus, so that the life of Jesus may also be manifested in our bodies. For we who live are always being given over to death for Jesus' sake, so that the life of*

Jesus also may be manifested in our mortal flesh. So death is at work in us, but life in you. . . . So we do not lose heart. Though our outer nature is wasting away, our inner nature is being renewed day by day. For this slight momentary affliction is preparing for us an eternal weight of glory beyond all comparison, as we look not to the things that are seen but to the things that are unseen. For the things that are seen are transient, but the things that are unseen are eternal. (2 CORINTHIANS 4:7-12, 16-18)

God is our refuge and strength, a very present help in trouble. Therefore we will not fear though the earth gives way, though the mountains be moved into the heart of the sea, though its waters roar and foam, though the mountains tremble at its swelling. Selah There is a river whose streams make glad the city of God, the holy habitation of the Most High. God is in the midst of her; she shall not be moved; God will help her when morning dawns. The nations rage, the kingdoms totter; he utters his voice, the earth melts. The LORD of hosts is with us; the God of Jacob is our fortress. Selah Come, behold the works of the LORD, how he has brought desolations on the earth. He makes wars cease to the end of the earth; he breaks the bow and shatters the spear; he burns the chariots with fire. "Be still, and know that I am God. I will be exalted among the nations, I will be exalted in the earth!" The LORD of hosts is with us; the God of Jacob is our fortress. Selah

PSALM 46:1-11, ESV

2

GOD WITH US

Burns covered 90 percent of thirteen-year-old Ben Willis's body. His parents, Scott and Janet, knew he would die. They said visiting Benny in intensive care, knowing he would not make it, was the hardest thing to face, harder than losing five other children in a fire on the freeway. "Thank God they died quickly." At the memorial service five caskets lined the front of the church (the youngest two were buried together). The bodies of Ben (thirteen), Joe (eleven), Sam (nine), Hank (seven), Elizabeth (three), and Peter (six weeks) rested on the very platform where Pastor Scott Willis regularly preached.

Perhaps you remember the story of their van exploding after hitting a piece of metal that dropped off a semi. In the memorial service the presiding pastor spoke of how Scott quoted Job 1:21: "Naked I came from my mother's womb, and naked shall I return. The LORD gave, and the LORD has taken away; blessed be the name of the LORD."

These modern-day Jobs blessed God from the eye of the storm, and we can't begin to imagine their grief and pain. In his book *Lament for a Son*, Nicholas Wolterstorff writes, "It's the neverness that is so painful. Never again to be here with us — never to sit with us at table, never to travel with us, never to laugh with us, never to cry with us, never to embrace us as he leaves for school, never to see his brothers and sister marry. All the rest of our lives we must live without him. Only our death can stop the pain of his death."[1]

Like Job, Scott and Janet Willis worshiped through their suffering. That is the test. Satan was convinced that suffering would put Job under, but innocent Job blessed God's name even when his wife advised him to curse God and die.

Chapter 1 of the book of Job reminds us that it is possible for the innocent to suffer. We have seen that God not only allows the storm but ultimately brings the storms, and yet he remains holy and altogether good. God is looking for worshipers who in suffering continue to worship him, bringing all their pain and agony to him, submitting everything to his ways and his will, blessing his character even when they feel like cursing his name. How wonderful it is as they join together with God's people in worship, though separated by a veil of tears.

If you are in the midst of a storm today, you will know that what was true for Job is true for you: While in the storm, it is hard to trust God. Trusting God seems as impossible as worshiping him. It's hard because God can seem so distant, his purposes so unclear. It's hard to trust someone you can't see. It's hard to trust the Lord when everything is in a state of chaos. It is hard to trust him when his love feels so weak or even absent. These strong feelings tear away at our faith, filling us with deep fear and, if we are honest, dark despondency. Job's despair was real. Although he didn't curse God, he cursed the day he was born. In his great lament recorded in chapter 3 he says, "Let the day perish on which I was born" (v. 3). "Or why was I not as a hidden stillborn child?" (v. 16).

In the storm we sometimes doubt that God is there. Or if he is, why doesn't he do something — why doesn't he answer us? Job says, "Behold, I go forward, but he is not there, and backward, but I do not perceive him; on the left hand when he is working, I do not behold him; he turns to the right hand, but I do not see him (23:8-

9). Everywhere Job looks, God can't be found, and pretty soon all hope is gone. Job says to God, "My hope has he pulled up like a tree" (19:10). Perhaps you have seen, as I have, a huge tree uprooted after a storm, with the whole root structure exposed to the morning sun. This massive tree, which yesterday was a symbol of strength, now is toppled, reminding us of the storm's power to uproot our lives — our faith, our souls and relationships.

When your life is toppled by one of the storms of life, it is easy to echo Job.

> *God has cast me into the mire, and I have become like dust and ashes. I cry to you for help and you do not answer me; I stand, and you only look at me. You have turned cruel to me; with the might of your hand you persecute me. You lift me up on the wind; you make me ride on it, and you toss me about in the roar of the storm. (30:19-22)*

Psalm 46 links our feelings to the truth of who God is and what he is up to in the storms of life. God hasn't abandoned us. He is sovereign over our storm, but verse 1 tells us he is present in our storm. "God is our refuge and strength, a very present help in trouble. Therefore we will not fear though the earth gives way, though the mountains be moved into the heart of the sea, though its waters roar and foam, though the mountains tremble at its swelling" (vv. 1-3).

I love the fact that Psalm 46 is all about God from start to finish. Notice how it begins and how it ends — with the fact that our God is with us! He is our refuge, our fortress. This truth is trumpeted from each of the three stanzas. The first verse of this song (vv. 1-3) has it at the beginning, so we would understand what this song is about. The second stanza (vv. 4-7) and the third (vv. 8-11) have it at the end.

It is significant that the writer starts with what we need in the storm, not with where we are. He starts with God and tells us three important things to remember about God when we are in the midst of a severe trial:

- He is our "refuge."
- He is our "strength."
- He is "a very present help in trouble."

This is who God *is*, not what he can be. These are statements of fact about our great God that are still true today, potent truths on which we can build our lives.

First, God is our "refuge," our shelter. Isaiah 25:4 says of God, "you have been . . . a shelter from the storm." That's the image — a shelter, a place of protection in the storm. God protects us from the dangers that surround us. Just about every year for the last twenty-two years, my family and I have gone to Horn Creek Ranch in Westcliffe, Colorado. When Laura and Bridget were eight and ten, we decided to climb Horn Peak, which is part of the Sangre de Cristo mountain range in southern Colorado. Horn Peak is 13,450 feet tall and as tough as any "fourteener" I have ever climbed. But up we went. Our girls made it all the way to the top, but we didn't have much time to rest and take in the majestic view of the surrounding peaks because a violent storm was blowing in just as we reached the summit.

Lightning flashed, and you could feel the electrical charge in the air. The wind was howling. It began to rain, then turned to sleet and finally hail and snow. Being far above the tree line, we were completely exposed. I grabbed the girls' hands, and with the help of a guide we literally ran down the face of the mountain looking for refuge. We needed a safe place from the fierce storm. Psalm 46 says God is that safe place. He is our protection, our refuge in the storm.

Second, God is our "strength." The storms wear us out; our bloodshot eyes burn because we have no more tears to give — we're cried out. We curl into the fetal position, groaning and wishing we would wake up and find out it was all a bad dream. The storms *reveal* our weakness, but God is our refuge. Storms *create* weakness, but God is our strength. Paul addressed this very thing when he talked about his thorn in the flesh in 2 Corinthians 12:9-10: "Therefore I will boast all the more gladly of my weaknesses, so that the power of Christ may rest upon me. For the sake of Christ, then, I am content with weaknesses, insults, hardships, persecutions, and calamities. For when I am weak, then I am strong."

Third, and this is the best news, God is "a very present help in trouble." What good is his shelter if you can't find it, and what good is his strength if you have to travel to heaven to get it? How awesome to be reminded in the storm that although we may not feel his presence, we have God's Word on it — "a very present help." God is right here; he is with us in the storm.

God is right at our side, easy to find, and ready to help in times of trouble. When I received the two phone calls I mentioned in the last chapter, the choking fear that gripped my soul was like nothing I have ever experienced in all my life.

The call about my mother's death came to me on May 9 when I was in the lobby of our church commons. Our preaching workshop had just ended, and in God's providence Sparky Pritchard, my small group leader from that workshop, was right there. I remember getting off the phone and walking over to him and telling him I needed a hug because I had just heard that my mom had unexpectedly passed away. Having Sparky there was just what my aching heart needed. He told me through tears that two years ago he received the same phone call concerning his mother's death. Of course we don't always have someone there with us. Perhaps you feel all alone in the midst of your storm. Well-meaning friends may parrot, "I know just how you feel," but deep down in your heart you know they don't have a clue.

Here is the beauty of verse 1. This is who God is in the storms of life. When you wonder if he is there, if he cares, or if he knows, if your feelings question God, verse 1 settles the matter. He is *here*, with strength to protect you in your storm. And if this God is your

God, he is your refuge, strength, and present helper as you run to him for shelter, as you take hold of his strength or ask for his help. And if you don't do this, your failure to turn to him or the force of your storm you are in will never change who God is. Verse 1 is not a set of imperatives that tells us what to do in the storm. It is not telling us to run for protection, grab his power, or acknowledge his presence. Rather verses 1-3 give us two fantastic statements that remind us who God is in the storm and what he brings to us in the storms of life — protection, strength, and help. We do not need to fear, and we will not be moved.

YOU NEED NOT FEAR

The imperative (though it's not actually a command, but the psalmist's conclusion) comes in verse 2, and it's just what we need to hear when we are in the storm. "Therefore we will not fear though the earth gives way." If God is our refuge, strength, and very present helper, what do we have to fear? Therefore, says the psalmist, "we will not fear." Fear is perhaps the most dominant emotion one faces when going through a storm. Chase down the "fear nots" in the Bible, and surrounding them you will find storms.

God spoke those words to Abraham when he feared that God wouldn't keep his word and give him an heir, and to Hagar after she left Ishmael to die in the wilderness. The people of Israel heard the same words when they stood before the Red Sea and saw the Egyptian chariots gaining ground. And some of us need to hear it again today. Fear not!

Lori's diagnosis came on December 11, 2002, two weeks before Christmas. Those very words printed on a Christmas card settled deep within her heart. "Fear not, for behold I bring you good news of great joy that will be for all the people. For unto you is born this day in the city of David a Savior, who is Christ the Lord" (Luke 2:10-11). When Lori woke up in the middle of the night, fear was hovering like a dark shadow over her soul. But so too was God's Word: "Fear not." God has not given us a spirit of fear but of power and love and self-control (see 2 Timothy 1:7). Be sure of this: God is not the author of our fear. Fear comes from the enemy as he presents the facts of our storm, emphasizing the negative, of course. He paints a dark picture of our future, all the time enticing us to doubt whether God is really in control, whether his Word is really true. Our foe takes us back to the implicit question he posed to Adam and Eve in the garden — "is God really good?"

When the earth gives way and mountains fall into the sea, when waters roar and foam (see Psalm 46:2-3), fear is a real possibility. But remember who God is, and let him chase away your fear. He is "our refuge and strength, a very present help in trouble." Fear not!

You Will Not Be Moved

When God is with you, you will not be overcome or defeated. In the second stanza of the song of Psalm 46 (vv. 4-7), the psalmist changes pictures — from the raging storm to the besieged city. The picture here is that of Jerusalem, the city of God, surrounded by an enemy. That is how Job felt in his storm except that it was God who had him encircled. He said, "His troops come on together; they have cast up their siege ramp against me and encamp around my tent" (19:12).

The besieged city of Jerusalem in verse 4 of Psalm 46 has a river running through it. That gracious provision of God meant everything to a people who were surrounded by an army. Defeat is certain if there is no water supply. Those who feel besieged by God are here reminded that he sends rivers of grace that bring gladness to our souls, allowing us to survive even when we feel as if we are on the verge of defeat.

In the first verse of the song we learn that God is with us; now we see that God is in the midst of his people (v. 5). We read in verse

7 that he is "the LORD of hosts", the captain of heaven's army. Remember what Jesus said to Peter after he cut off Malchus' ear? In essence, "I could call twelve legions of angels. So put your sword away" (Matthew 26:53). Twelve legions (seventy-two thousand soldiers) are a lot of reinforcements! Remember, one angel (the angel of the Lord) wiped out 185,000 Assyrian soldiers (see 2 Kings 19:35)! The Lord of hosts is with us; in the midst of his people he is helping us against the raging forces, and he will not let us be overcome. The word "moved" in verse 5 means "shaken or overthrown." God's presence in the storm will not let his followers fall in defeat. God can do this because he is all-powerful and works on our behalf.

Verse 6 goes on to say, "The nations rage, the kingdoms totter; he utters his voice, the earth melts." His power is seen here in his word. Remember, it was by his word that he created everything out of nothing. Verse 6 tells us that by the power of his word, "the earth melts." Jesus commanded the storm, "'Peace! Be still!' And the wind ceased, and there was a great calm" (Mark 4:39). His word is powerful, and so are his actions. He brings "desolations" (v. 8), and his power "makes wars cease to the end of the earth; he breaks the bow and shatters the spear; he burns the chariots with fire" (v. 9).

All of our military might, with our tanks and fighter jets and rockets and missiles and warships, is no match for God's power. He has brought victory to his people in the past, and he can do it for you today. He defeated the nations that raged against him, and he can take on your raging storm.

Many people have gone through a storm only to see their faith shipwrecked. The stakes are high. The storms can drive us into God's protective care, or they can bring us to the place where in our pain we walk away from him, no longer trusting in his promises. Jesus said this would happen in the Parable of the Sower. Remember the seed that fell on the rocky ground? "And these are the ones sown on rocky ground: the ones who, when they hear the word, immediately receive it with joy. And they have no root in themselves, but endure for a while; then, when tribulation or persecution arises on account of the word, immediately they fall away" (Mark 4:16-17).

Everything is moving in this Psalm — the earth, the mountains, the waters, nations and kingdoms. But because God is with his people, because God is in their midst, they will not be moved. The same can be true for God's people today. Has a storm shaken you or knocked you off your feet? The one who makes wars to cease and one day will stop them for all time can give you peace and keep you on your feet, strong and steady, unmoved, fighting the good fight of faith.

SOME CONCLUDING THOUGHTS

When God is your refuge and strength, you need not fear. When God is your refuge and strength, you will not be defeated. When God is your refuge and strength, you can trust him! The picture we are given in the final stanza (vv. 8-11) explains further what it looks like to fight in faith. It is a picture of a believer who is quietly trusting God. "Be still, and know that I am God" (v. 10). The command is not to be still and know why God is doing this, or to be still and know how to get out of this mess, or to be still and weep for yourself, but to be still and know that God is God.

The Hebrew word translated "be still" literally means to let your hands drop. I think of Lori's and my first date (a double date) twenty-five years ago when she blindfolded me and my friend. She was leading us through a park, pretending that we were stepping over logs and going under branches, but her laughter let us know we were being had. If you have ever been blindfolded, I can almost guarantee you that your hands were in the same position mine were — straight out in front, so that nothing whacked you in the head. We are vulnerable when we can't see, and our natural reaction is to put our hands up in order to protect ourselves. We look like a walking mummy. God says, "I am with you in the storm. I know you can't see me, and you aren't sure where I am taking you, but trust me. Let me guide you to the refuge. Let me give you strength. Cease your striving. Put your arms down, take my hand, and let me lead you. Trust me."

Ken Gire, in his excellent book *The Weathering Grace of God*, observes that most injuries during an earthquake come when people try to escape the quake. They slip, they fall, or they are hit with falling debris or flying glass. So the first rule of earthquake safety is to stay still.[2] That was Job's problem at the beginning. He said in 3:26, "I am not at ease, nor am I quiet; I have no rest, but trouble comes." But by the end Job was still, with his hand clasped over his mouth; he was silent (40:4-5). Then in the final chapter he said that in his stillness he now knew God: "I had heard of you by the hearing of the ear, but now my eye sees you" (42:5).

When you can't see through the dark clouds of your storm, remember that it is stillness that gives perspective. Joni Eareckson Tada puts it like this:

> That God is a part of the problem of suffering may not complicate matters after all. How or to what extent he's involved in the problem is not the question. The point is, he is the answer, and we need him. In suffering, God does not give the blueprint, but himself. God is a God of love, and anyone who's in love gives himself. God doesn't give a list of answers; he is the Answer.[3]

I have been musing over why God reveals himself in Psalm 46 as "the God of Jacob . . . our fortress" (vv. 7, 11). Why not as the God of Abraham or Isaac or simply as Jehovah? Is it to help us understand that amidst the storms of life, God, our fortress, our high tower of protection, comes to us personally, protecting weak and imperfect men and women like Jacob who seemed to be on the run and in trouble and in constant need of God's protection? Or was it because in Jacob's storm he wrestled with God all night until God immobilized him, touching his hip, forcing him to be still (see Genesis 31:22-32)? Or is it because God kept his promise to Jacob to be with him so that through his family God would send the promised Messiah, Immanuel, God with us? That promised one "passed through the heavens, Jesus, the Son of God" (Hebrews 4:14). Verses 15-16 of Hebrews 4 go on to say, "We do not have a high priest who is unable to sympathize with our weaknesses, but one who in every respect has been tempted as we are, yet without sin. Let us then with confidence draw near to the throne of grace, that we may receive mercy and find grace to help in time of need." Be still!

Remember Peter walking on the waves? I can just see it. Peter sees Jesus walking on the water, and before he knows what happened, he has stepped out of the boat, and he too is walking on water. He laughs a nervous laugh and cries out for all to hear. Can you believe it? The "rock" is walking on water. But then his eyes shift to the waves, and all of sudden he realizes the water is choppy, and he takes his eyes off Jesus. And when he does, he starts to drown and cries out, "Lord, have mercy. Save me!"

Three kinds of people are reading this book — which are you? Some of you don't know that Jesus was called Immanuel, the ultimate expression of God with us. Psalm 46 points ahead to Christ, who came in the flesh to be your Savior, to save you from the ultimate storm that's going to come to all of us when we stand before God on Judgment Day. And at that time he's going to ask each of us, "What did you do with my Son?" Maybe you're not ready for that question. I say to you, as Jesus told the apostle Peter, fix your eyes on Christ, call out to him for mercy, and in faith take hold of Christ, trusting in him alone for your salvation.

Some of us are in the storm, and we're walking on waves, and our eyes are focused. To you I say, keep your eyes trained on Christ. And yet others are saying, "I'm sinking. I'm not far from drowning." I remember greeting people at the end of a service after preaching on Psalm 46. Someone came up to me who I knew was going through a difficult time, and he held his fingers about a quarter of an inch apart and said, "I am this far from going under." The Word of God comes to you and says, don't let fear dominate. Don't let the storm shipwreck your faith. Keep your eyes on Christ. Be still and know God. He's your refuge and strength, your very present help right now.

Be still and remember who God is. He is our shelter and strength in the storm. He is with us when we're besieged by an enemy. He makes wars to cease, and he will be exalted. Exalt him now as you trust him to be and do what he promises. "Be strong and courageous. Do not fear or be in dread of them, for it is the LORD your God who goes with you. He will not leave you or forsake you" (Deuteronomy 31:6).

SCRIPTURES FOR REFLECTION

Be merciful to me, O God, be merciful to me, for in you my soul takes refuge; in the shadow of your wings I will take refuge, till the storms of destruction pass by. (PSALM 57:1)

For you have been a stronghold to the poor, a stronghold to the needy in his distress, a shelter from the storm and a shade from the heat. (ISAIAH 25:4)

You keep him in perfect peace whose mind is stayed on you, because he trusts in you. Trust in the LORD forever, for the LORD GOD is an everlasting rock. (ISAIAH 26:3-4)

Consider him who endured from sinners such hostility against himself, so that you may not grow weary or fainthearted. In your struggle against sin you have not yet resisted to the point of shedding your blood. And have you forgotten the exhortation that addresses you as sons? "My son, do not regard lightly the discipline of the Lord, nor be weary when reproved by him. For the Lord disciplines the one he loves, and chastises every son whom he receives." It is for discipline that you have to endure. God is treating you as sons. For what son is there whom his father does not discipline? If you are left without discipline, in which all have participated, then you are illegitimate children and not sons. Besides this, we have had earthly fathers who disciplined us and we respected them. Shall we not much more be subject to the Father of spirits and live? For they disciplined us for a short time as it seemed best to them, but he disciplines us for our good, that we may share his holiness. For the moment all discipline seems painful rather than pleasant, but later it yields the peaceful fruit of righteousness to those who have been trained by it.

HEBREWS 12:3-11, ESV

3

GOD'S PURPOSES
FOR THE STORMS

In the midst of the storms that rage, the question *why?* thunders forth! *Why me? Why my child? Why my marriage? Why my job? Why now?* Job asked, "Why won't you leave me alone — even for a moment? Have I sinned? What have I done to you, O watcher of all humanity? Why have you made me your target?" (Job 7:19-20, NLT).

Nancy Guthrie, in her outstanding book *Holding on to Hope*, writes, "From the depths of your soul, don't you hunger to see the bigger picture, to see a purpose for your pain? My husband and I do. Today we wonder why again?"[1]

The Guthries' storm had to do with their first daughter, Hope. After discovering some seemingly small problems at birth, the Guthries learned through a geneticist that Hope had a metabolic disorder called Zellweger syndrome. As a result Hope was unable to rid her cells of toxins. Her system would slowly shut down, giving her less than six months to live. No treatments, no cure, no survivors!

At the time that she was writing her book and after taking medical measures to insure that they could no longer have children,

Nancy found out that "miraculously" she was pregnant. That explains her question, "Why again?" Little Gabriel was born with the same condition and lived one day short of six months! Situations like this cause us to shake our heads and sometimes our fists at God as we wonder why he would allow them.

As we tackle God's purposes for storms, we will see why James put the word *joy* so close to the word *trial*: "count it all joy . . . when you meet trials of various kinds" (James 1:2). When I think about the tragic deaths of four men in the church where I am a pastor, I am reminded that I have no answer to the looming question, *Why?* I don't know why God would take Dr. Rich Dominguez in his prime, through a car accident, leaving behind a wife and nine children. I have nothing to say to Jeff Perrine's two children as to why their godly father died after suffering from brain tumors. I don't know why the Lord would take home his effective servant Jonathan Thigpen through ALS, or why Dr. Andrew Chong in his early fifties would have his life snuffed out by pancreatic cancer. (I realize few of the readers of this book knew these men, but they stand for so many others who suffer in a similar way.) I don't know why teens die in car accidents or why beautiful children drown or are stillborn.

If we go back to the book of Job, we see that Job is crying out for an answer. He wants someone who will stand between him and God, someone to answer his questions. When God finally speaks in the closing chapters, Job never gets his answer. In fact, what he gets is anything but an answer. God asks him one question after another, leaving Job speechless. God never said, "Job, I have a good book I would like you to read—it has your name on it. Pay particular attention to chapters 1 and 2—they should prove very helpful for you!" Job never got his questions answered, and neither will we. You may have the same driving question that he and so many others have had, but I am afraid that the answer is wrapped in the mystery of God's providence. Having said that, I want to assure you that when we understand God's general purposes for the storms of life, we will be immensely helped as we wrestle with the particulars of our own storm.

Answering the question of purpose is different from answering the why question. The why question, when it is thrown up to God, has a specific situation in mind, and the question is usually very personal. The purpose question is a big-picture question that deals with the subject of suffering, not the specifics of *my* suffering.

The writer to the book of Hebrews feared that his brothers and sisters in Christ, in the midst of the storms of life, might drift away from the faith. He was afraid they were going to bow out of the race that God had charted for them. We know from verse 3 of chapter 12 that growing weary and giving up were real possibilities for his friends. Maybe that is where you are — ready to throw in the towel and call it quits.

Maybe you're like Job, whose great losses (see Chapter 1 of this book) were followed by more physical suffering (Chapter 2). Maybe like Nancy and her husband, your grief has come to the point where you say, "God, won't you relent?" Job said in essence, "God, I feel like you're pushing me under" (see 30:22-23). Job apparently felt like a scrawny kid who was being held underwater by the local bully. "God, give me some air." In your suffering you may find yourself discouraged, depressed, angry, weak, totally depleted, unable to go forward. God has a good word for us — a word that will help us respond to the storms. And for those of us who are sailing under sunny skies, he has an important word to prepare us for the gales that will come. And they will come!

STORMS DRAW US TO CHRIST

God's storms are meant to draw or move us to Christ and his sufferings, making us more like Christ. Listen again to verses 3-4 of Hebrews 12: "Consider him who endured from sinners such hostility against himself, so that you may not grow weary or fainthearted.

In your struggle against sin you have not yet resisted to the point of shedding your blood."

Similar to Psalm 46, which ends exhorting us to cease our striving, to be still and know God, the writer of Hebrews tells us to "consider" Christ. That's the only command in this whole section, and it means to think of or compare. It's a call to carefully assess Jesus, specifically his sufferings. It means to consider him who endured from sinners hostility to the point of shedding his own blood!

We know from verses 1-2 that if we are going to run with endurance the race that God has laid out for each of us, if we are to finish well, we will have to throw off the sin that so easily entangles us and keep our eyes on Jesus. When you think about fixing your eyes on Jesus, where does your mind's eye take you? Is he lying in a manger, teaching in the temple, walking on water, healing the deaf and blind? Do you see him being transfigured on the mountain, feeding five thousand, reigning in heaven, suffering on the cross?

Hebrews 12 calls us to fix our eyes on Jesus during the storms of life. He is the Suffering Servant who came to save us, the one who endured the cross, despising its shame, the one who devoted his life entirely to the will of his Father, the one who gave his life for you and me. He was falsely accused in a bogus trial. He was hated and despised, beaten and bruised, mocked and spit at, nailed to a cross where he hung naked in humiliation. The perfect, innocent Son of God was crucified with common criminals! Have you ever thought about the fact that Christianity is the only faith that has a God who suffers? Hebrews 12 is saying, when you suffer, when you are in anguish, let the anguish and suffering drive you to see Christ and his suffering. In other words, let your sufferings take you to the Suffering Servant.

That is exactly what happened to Dr. Andrew Chong. He sent many of his friends an e-mail on March 2, 2003. Here are some excerpts:

God visited me last Thursday night, while I was in bed. I had not been able to sleep that night and remembered getting up to use the bathroom around 3 a.m. . . . I did not see a vision, or feel the flutter of angel wings, or hear a still small voice. But I had sweet communion with Him, like a child with his father. . . . I remembered words from Him flooding my soul. The words did not enter my ears, but I felt like my mouth was wide open, and I was eating them up. In the last few weeks that I had been in pain, I had asked God over and over, "Why are you allowing me to suffer this pain? It is of no benefit to you, or me. This is so meaningless!"

But that night, He came and explained to me why. He knows the pain I was going through, but He wants me to experience this pain so that I can understand more fully the pain that His dear Son endured. . . . I have been a Christian for a long time. I have accepted God's gift of His Son on the cross for my sins. But I had never fully understood why Jesus had to endure that agony on the cross. That night I understood why. Enduring the pain and suffering was part of the price He paid for us, since pain was part of the punishment for sin. I also finally understood the awfulness of sin; it leads to pain and death, which I would have to endure in hell had it not been for my Savior. Having this pain from pancreatic cancer reminds me of the awfulness of sin and its consequences, and allows me to appreciate more fully what it cost God to redeem us. . . . He put everything in such clear perspective, so that I could understand the whole panorama of his great redemptive plan for man. I remember thinking, let this last forever. . . . During the visit, He did not indicate to me if He was going to heal me. It did not occur to me to ask Him. At the time, it did not seem to be that important.

The second chapter of Hebrews gives many reasons for Jesus' suffering.

He suffered to taste death for all of us (v. 9), and his sacrifice in our place crowns him with glory and honor.

He suffered to become the perfect Savior (v. 10). He was sinless, but as the sinless, suffering Son of God he became the perfect Savior. Perfect because he knew no sin and perfect because he understands our suffering and can help us. "For because he himself has suffered when tempted, he is able to help those who are being tempted" (2:18; cf. 4:15-16).

Many followers of Jesus Christ would say that unless God had shouted to them in their suffering or through pain had driven them to their knees, they never would have seen their need for his mercy and grace. Hebrews 2:14 says that Jesus had to suffer death in order to destroy the power of death and the devil and to free us from our sin. If you do not have a relationship with God, I can tell you the main reason you are going through a storm right now — God desires a relationship with you, made possible through Jesus' sufferings. The apostle Peter puts it this way: "For Christ also suffered once for sins, the righteous for the unrighteous, that he might bring us to God" (1 Peter 3:18a). Let your storm drive you to God's Son!

Think about it — God *suffered* pain to bring you to himself, and God *uses* pain to bring you to himself. In his book *The Problem of Pain* C. S. Lewis says that suffering is God's megaphone to get our attention: "God whispers to us in our pleasures, speaks in our conscience, but shouts in our pains: it is His megaphone to rouse a deaf world."[2] In your storm consider him who suffered for you.

STORMS MAKE US MORE LIKE CHRIST

The word *discipline* shows up nine times in this passage. The Lord's discipline is the language that the writer uses to talk about the storms of life. For that reason we need to understand what is involved in the word *discipline* and in the phrase *the Lord's discipline*. When I do a word association with the word *discipline*, my mind goes back to a wooden cooking spoon in my mother's hand ready to be applied to my backside for punishment and instruction. But that's only half of the meaning. Discipline involves punishment that leads to correction, but it also has to do with training and instruction. The word translated "discipline" comes from the same root word for child and centers on the training of a child. "The word is a broad term, signifying whatever parents and teachers do to train, correct, cultivate, and educate children in order to help them develop and mature as they ought."[3] In Ephesians 6:4 fathers are commanded to bring up their children in the "discipline [training] and instruction of the Lord", and the Greek word translated "discipline" is the same word we find in Hebrews 12.

Implicit in the broad meaning of the word is an understanding that the Lord's discipline can come for different reasons. Sometimes discipline will come as a result of sin in our lives, bringing the Lord's correction. We should always remember that Christ suffered the *punishment* for our sins on the cross. As believers, we may suffer the consequences for our sin, but never the punishment. We may also suffer because of someone else's sin. And sometimes we just plain suffer — like the blind man in John 9. "Who sinned," the disciples asked, "this man or his parents?" Jesus answered that it was neither. Then why was he blind? ". . . that the works of God might be displayed in him" (vv. 2-3).

The words "my son" (a quotation from Proverbs 3:11-12) in Hebrews 12 give us the important context surrounding the Lord's discipline — a loving relationship. God calls us sons, and he is our Father who knows and does what is best. In fact, in verses 5-9 we find nine references to either son, father, or children. Look at verses 7b-8: "God is treating you as sons. For what son is there whom his father does not discipline? If you are left without discipline, in which all have participated, then you are illegitimate children and not sons."

The fact is, God's storms, his discipline in our lives, is in effect a birth certificate that he hands to us to say, "You belong to me." It authenticates our relationship as son or daughter. I discipline my children, and no one else's, and the fact that I discipline them shows they are my children! Seen in its context, we understand that the Lord's discipline shows us God's love. That is surprising because when we are in the storm we don't usually say, "Thanks, Lord, for showing me your love — I love you too!" We are more likely to question in the vein of the psalmist:

> *"Will the Lord spurn forever, and never again be favorable? Has his steadfast love forever ceased? Are his promises at an end for all time? Has God forgotten to be gracious? Has he in anger shut up his compassion?" (77:7-9)*

The storms don't feel loving, but when we remember what God is doing in and through them, and when we remember that abandonment or indifference is the opposite of love, we will see the storms for what they really are — God's gracious instruments to draw us to him and make us like him.

THE WARNING

The warning follows in the passage because we so often allow our feelings to redefine God's character when we are in the storm. Here are the two things to stay away from when you are going through a storm, for they will certainly short-circuit God's purpose: Don't regard the Lord's discipline lightly, and don't grow weary.

To treat something lightly means to regard something as having little value. What a temptation it is to say to God, "This makes no sense — it's useless. What good can come out of this? God, I don't think you know what you're doing." Don't conclude that the Lord's discipline is worthless. It has great value because of what it brings and great value because of what it does. Don't miss the opportunity to grow. Remember, God does great things in the midst of hard times.

The second warning is to not grow weary. The core idea here is giving up from exhaustion. The force of the storm has worn you out. You have been under the weight of it, and finally you just collapse. You've had it; you can't take it any longer. You know that 1 Corinthians 10:13 says that God is faithful and won't let you be tested beyond what you are able, but you are convinced that God has lost track of your storm. You have fallen off his radar screen, and so you are throwing in the towel. You're calling it quits. You drift away as you drop out of the race.

Speaking of our fathers, the writer says, "For they disciplined us for a short time as it seemed best to them, but he [the Lord] disciplines us for our good, that we may share his holiness" (v. 10). There it is, there's the purpose for our storm — to share in God's holiness. We know this is truly important because verse 14 says that without holiness we can't see God.

This is fascinating. We know from other passages that without Christ's suffering we would never be reconciled to God, and here we read that without suffering there is no way to share in God's holiness. Holiness is imputed to us through Christ. That is, he gives us his holiness when we trust in him as Savior. He not only takes away our sin — he gives us his holiness, his righteousness (see 2 Corinthians 5:21). We understand from Hebrews 12 that in the midst of suffering and through suffering he makes us holy more and more by degree, and finally in whole when someday we will see him face-to-face in heaven.

Suffering can make you holy. Isn't that James's point in James 1:2-4? "Count it all joy, my brothers, when you meet trials of various kinds, for you know that the testing of your faith produces steadfastness. And let steadfastness have its full effect, that you may be perfect and complete, lacking in nothing." That's holiness, and to get there James says we need endurance or steadfastness; and to get endurance we need a resistant force, which strengthens faith. That force is called a trial, a storm if you will — the Lord's discipline. Paul says the same thing in 2 Corinthians 4:8-10: "We are afflicted in every way, but not crushed; perplexed, but not driven to despair; persecuted, but not forsaken; struck down, but not destroyed; always carrying in the body the death of Jesus, so that the life of Jesus may also be manifested in our bodies."

Do you see how it works? Trials test us, refine us, polish us. The storms work on our character like a sculptor with marble. Everything that is not like Christ is chipped away. If we are going to share in God's holiness and reap the peaceful fruit of righteousness, we need to let God chip away and hack away at everything that isn't like Christ. Are you willing to let God do that? Look at the response that we are called to make in this passage.

EMBRACE THE CROSS

Verse 7 of Hebrews 12 calls us to "endure." The word used means "to remain under." We need to embrace the storm and remain under its force, allowing it to do God's good work in our lives. We must choose to remain under its crushing weight, letting it drive us to Christ, allowing it to drive out all that is not Christ. In the movie *The Passion of the Christ*, Mel Gibson vividly portrayed this point as Christ is seen wrapping his arms around the cross. In fact, Gibson has one of the criminals mock Jesus for embracing his cross. We need endurance so we can stay under the storm, embracing the cross.

EMBRACE HIS RULE

We need to submit, to place ourselves under God's authority (v. 9). We are thus saying, "God, you are God. You are sovereign over every area of my life. Everything that I have is from you, and you can do with it what you will, and I will bless your name." We need to submit and in so doing embrace his rule.

We need the proper perspective that says, *This storm is for my good* (vv. 10-11). The contrast here is between parents who did what "*seemed* best" (emphasis mine) and God who "disciplines us for our good." He makes no mistakes, no miscalculations. He always disciplines us for our good. Let me mention some of the good things that happen through the storms of life, according to God's Word.

• It is a good thing when his discipline reminds us that we are loved and that we are his children (Hebrews 12:6).

• It is a good thing when we are able to comfort those in affliction with the comfort we have ourselves received from God (2 Corinthians 1:3-7).

• It is a good thing when storms make us more dependent on God and less on ourselves. There is nothing like a storm to show us just how weak we are and how strong God is. That is Paul's point about his thorn in the flesh in 2 Corinthians 12 — we will say more about this in Chapter 4.

• It is a good thing when others are strengthened through someone else's perseverance (Philippians 1:12-14) — more on this in Chapter 5.

• It is also a good thing when the genuineness of our faith is tested so that it brings greater glory to Christ (1 Peter 1:7).

The storms make us hungrier for heaven — and that is a good thing. Storms wean us from this world; we come to love it less. The things of this world, the creature comforts that we pursued so passionately in earlier times, simply don't do it for us anymore. I have never heard someone going through a storm say to me, "You know, having a big house and a nice car and a great job is making things so much easier for me." When you are being pummeled by a storm, those things simply don't matter — and that is a good thing, a very good thing. This is the perspective we must have if we are to share in God's holiness (Hebrews 12:10). The storms are for our good. Can you say that about the specific funnel cloud you are in right now?

The proper perspective leads to a proper attitude, which is, *I want to be trained by this storm*. Verse 11 says it yields "the peaceful fruit of righteousness" to those who are willing to be "trained", to those who embrace it, who stay under its weight, who desire to grow in grace. How is your attitude?

The proper expectations are crucial. Expect the storms to come, and expect them to be "painful" (v. 11); they're not going to be pleasant. But remember, they won't last forever — the storms are for this life, not the next. We discipline our young children for a time and then no more (v. 10). That is why Paul could call his affliction "slight [and] momentary" (2 Corinthians 4:17).

Ken Gire closes his book *The Weathering Grace of God* with an illustration from the life of van Gogh. Van Gogh was a pastor in a small coal-mining town. In 1877 he preached a sermon about the pilgrimage of life. He told the weary miners that they were strangers on this earth, fellow travelers on their way home. Van Gogh talked about the joys and sorrows of that journey, then used a painting of an autumn landscape to illustrate his point. In the distance a row of mountains stood in hazy dusk. The peaks displayed the setting sun, whose rays touched the underbellies of clouds, turning common silver to gold, and gold to royal purple. A road cut through the landscape to a distant mountain. Crowning the mountain was a city, glowing in the sunset.

On the road a weary traveler, with staff in hand, encountered an angel who had been placed there to encourage those on their way to the eternal city. Then Van Gogh gave the words that he imagined might have passed between them.

The traveler asked, "Does the road go uphill all the way?" The angel answered, "Yes, to the very end." The traveler then inquired, "Will the journey take all day long?" The angel replied, "From morn 'til night, my friend."

The traveler journeyed on, sorrowful yet rejoicing. Sorrowful because the road was so steep and long. Rejoicing because he was ever drawing closer to the destination that was home to his deepest longings.

As he continued to climb, a quiet prayer rose from his lips: "Then I shall be more and more tired — but also nearer and nearer to thee."

Van Gogh's tale is moving, but Hebrews 12 gives us someone far better than an angel — the Son of God. He meets us in our suffering and says in essence, "Consider my suffering for your sake. Hang on to my Word. Embrace and endure your suffering — it is meant for good, that you might share in my holiness. I am present with you. I am your refuge and strength, a very present help in trouble. I will walk by your side all the way to the celestial city. I will never leave you or forsake you. I will help you through the storm — I will get you home by nightfall."

GOD MOVES IN A MYSTERIOUS WAY

God moves in a mysterious way
His wonders to perform;
He plants His footsteps in the sea,
And rides upon the storm.

Deep in unfathomable mines
Of never-failing skill
He treasures up His bright designs,
And works His sovereign will.

Ye fearful saints, fresh courage take;
The clouds ye so much dread
Are big with mercy, and will break
With blessings on your head.

Judge not the Lord by feeble sense,
But trust Him for His grace;
Behind a frowning providence
He hides a smiling face.

His purposes will ripen fast,
Unfolding every hour;
The bud may have a bitter taste,
But sweet will be the flower.

GOD IN THE STORM

Blind unbelief is sure to err,
And scan His work in vain;
God is His own interpreter,
And He will make it plain.
WILLIAM COWPER (1731-1800)

SCRIPTURES FOR REFLECTION

"The LORD sits enthroned over the flood; the Lord sits enthroned as king forever. May the LORD give strength to his people! May the Lord bless his people with peace!"   (PSALM 29:10-11)

Since we are surrounded by so great a cloud of witnesses, let us also lay aside every weight, and sin which clings so closely, and let us run with endurance the race that is set before us, looking to Jesus, the founder and perfecter of our faith, who for the joy that was set before him endured the cross, despising the shame, and is seated at the right hand of the throne of God. Consider him who endured from sinners such hostility against himself, so that you may not grow weary or fainthearted.   (HEBREWS 12:1-3)

"I have said these things to you, that in me you may have peace. In the world you will have tribulation. But take heart; I have overcome the world."   (JOHN 16:33)

In this you rejoice, though now for a little while, if necessary, you have been grieved by various trials, so that the tested genuineness of your faith — more precious than gold that perishes though it is tested by fire — may be found to result in praise and glory and honor at the revelation of Jesus Christ. Though you have not seen him, you love him. Though you do not now see him, you believe in him and rejoice with joy that is inexpressible and filled with glory, obtaining the outcome of your faith, the salvation of your souls.   (1 PETER 1:6-9)

So to keep me from being too elated by the surpassing greatness of the revelations, a thorn was given me in the flesh, a messenger of Satan to harass me, to keep me from being too elated. Three times I pleaded with the Lord about this, that it should leave me. But he said to me, "My grace is sufficient for you, for my power is made perfect in weakness." Therefore I will boast all the more gladly of my weaknesses, so that the power of Christ may rest upon me. For the sake of Christ, then, I am content with weaknesses, insults, hardships, persecutions, and calamities. For when I am weak, then I am strong.

2 CORINTHIANS 12:7-10, ESV

4

THE GOD WHO PROVIDES

I want to share the story of a friend whom I met almost twenty years ago. David has been through an unbelievable storm, and God has provided for him all the way through! David shared his story of grace last year in my church. I will let him tell it:

My story is about God and his grace. It is about his mercy and forgiveness. I guess the best place to start is in the beginning — my beginning. Most of my memories begin when my mom and dad were getting separated. I was about five years old. For the next year or so I watched my parents fight over my brother and me as their marriage disintegrated. Since I had been living with my dad, and my brother with my mom, the judge decided to keep it that way.

My mom came from a Roman Catholic background, and my dad was Jewish, but neither of them practiced their faith. That explains why they didn't push either on us boys. I was able to form my own opinions on how to live and succeed. My main source of information other than school was probably TV and friends. At some point I realized my dad wasn't going to be influential in my life. So I decided I would raise myself. I grew up without a father around other than to belittle, punish, or scare me. Even though I followed the world's standards, I still tried to hold onto some moral ground. I wouldn't try drugs. I wouldn't have premarital sex. I'd be good to others. I'd treat other people well. As I got into my teen years, one by one most of those standards fell because I had no reason to hold onto them.

When I was sixteen, a few months into my junior year of high school, I saw absolutely no hope, no future. It got so bad, I even put a loaded pistol in my mouth with my finger on the trigger. For some reason all I thought of at that moment was my mom and dad finding me and being hurt. So I told my dad I needed help. He said I'd be okay — don't worry about it. Then I told him I was running away. He told me he'd stop me. Why I don't know. I was sixteen with what seemed like the weight of the world on my shoulders.

Then the worst thing that could ever happen happened. I blamed all my pain and my hurt, rightly or wrongly, on my father. I said to myself, *If he hits me again, I will fight back*. He did about ten days later, and I shot and killed him. Three days later I was arrested and confessed. On October 1, 1986, I was sent to DuPage County Youth Home. The very next day a man gave me a Bible and said, "You might want to read somewhere in Matthew or John." I started in Matthew and read all the way through the middle of Acts in fourteen days. In fact, in six weeks I had read the Bible from cover to cover. On October 15, 1986, the Lord woke me up. I knew Christ was real. I was in awe that the God of this world gave up everything for me, a sinner. John 3:16 came alive. John 1:12 told me that I would be a child of God if I just received him.

I realized that Christ was what I had been searching for all my life. So in a small dark room with no future and no hope, I confessed my sins to God and gave my life to Christ, surrendering my life to him. And in an instant I had a hope, a future, everlasting life, and most importantly, Christ in my life.

Shortly thereafter I met Pastor Maillefer, and he began to disciple me, making sure I was rooted, grounded, which was good for the storms that lay ahead. Yes, Christ had forgiven me, but there were still consequences for my actions. After two years of court proceedings I pled guilty, and the judge sentenced me to thirty years in prison. I was a skinny, eighteen-year-old, suburban white boy being sent to prison. At first glance one might think I was a lost cause. However, the Holy Spirit's comfort and protection got me through. I never got pressured to join a gang. I never got ridiculed for my faith. I saw extortion, dirty cops, stabbings, gang fights, and riots and sometimes was almost in the middle of them. Yet Christ guided me through it all.

Christ had told me that whatever door I walked through, whatever door closed behind me, whatever door locked behind me, he would be with me. He would *always* be with me. Amidst the violence, the hatred, the total lack of regard for decency, God was building me up for his use. And throughout many years in prison God kept me. He also allowed me to study the Bible, lead Bible studies, witness, and just be used by him. Throughout the storms that raged in my life, mostly brought on by myself, Christ brought me through.

After I was released, he didn't leave me or forsake me. He said he'd go everywhere with me, and he has. God has blessed me with good Christian friends who invited me into their homes as one of the family, for which I am thankful. I know that I am blessed. The Lord has also enabled me to get a good job. He's blessed me with a mom who loves me. He put me in a good church and has blessed me beyond belief, so much so that I could go on forever.

I realize not everybody's comfortable with what I'm saying. I understand somebody might have been a victim of a crime, or someone in their family has been, or maybe they know somebody who has been. Some may feel or think that I don't deserve to be free, alive, or maybe even changed. Whatever your thoughts are, my goal is not to make you feel uncomfortable, nor is it to alienate those with whom I have become friends. I just ask that you try and remember Paul's words in 1 Corinthians 6:9-11:

> *Do you not know that the unrighteous will not inherit the kingdom of God? Do not be deceived: neither the sexually immoral, nor idolaters, nor adulterers, nor men who practice homosexuality, nor thieves, nor the greedy, nor drunkards, nor revilers, nor swindlers will not inherit the kingdom of God. And such were some of you. But you were washed, you were sanctified, you were justified in the name of the Lord Jesus Christ and by the Spirit of our God.*

I give my testimony to give God the glory. Finally, you may ask yourself why I would give my testimony knowing that my life would be much easier without saying a word. Well, God in his grace and mercy completely changed me. He changed my life. And his life-changing power can change yours. If one person today has his or her life changed, my difficulties will be worth it. Thank you, and God bless.

David's letters from prison read like epistles, always praising and pointing others to God. He's been a good friend and a great example of God's powerful grace. By God's grace may he and all of us finish well!

David's story from beginning to the end is all about the sufficiency and power of God's grace in the midst of unbelievable storms. The apostle Paul, who had a similar experience, writes:

> *I thank him who has given me strength, Christ Jesus our Lord . . . though formerly I was a blasphemer, persecutor, and insolent opponent. But I received mercy because I had acted ignorantly in unbelief, and the grace of our Lord overflowed for me with the faith and love that are in Christ Jesus. (1 Timothy 1:12-14)*

My prayer for you is that you will come to know more and more about the overflowing, powerful grace of God — God's provision for your storms.

THE SUFFICIENCY OF GRACE IN PAUL'S STORM

We know from 2 Corinthians 12 that Paul had an unusual experience.

> *I know a man in Christ who fourteen years ago was caught up to the third heaven — whether in the body or out of the body I do not know, God knows. And I know that this man was caught up into paradise — whether in the body or out of the body I do not know, God knows — and he heard things that cannot be told, which man may not utter. (vv 2-4)*

I don't know about you, but if I had that kind of an experience, I would be talking about it. Isn't it interesting that rather than boast in this vision and revelation of the Lord, Paul boasts about the thorn that was given to him afterwards. We know from verses 7-8 that the reason God gave him that thorn was to keep him humble, to keep him from being elated or conceited after having had this incredible experience. What we know about the thorn is this:

• He'd had it for fourteen years (cf. vv. 2, 7).

• We know that the thorn was given to him by God. It doesn't say that explicitly in verse 7, but the passive voice implies that. Scholars call this the divine passive. God sent the thorn.

• We know the source: The thorn came through "a messenger of Satan" (v. 7).

• We believe that this probably had to do with his body — his flesh. Scott Hafemann writes in his commentary on 2 Corinthians that Paul is not interested in the medical diagnosis of his weakness, but in its theological origin, its cause, and its purpose.[1]

• We know it was difficult — it harassed him, and it caused him to repeatedly pray to God to take it away.

PAUL'S PRAYER

Note that Paul prayed that God would take the thorn in his flesh away. Three times (maybe more) Paul prayed about his thorn. When you are in a storm or trial, it is natural to ask God to take it away. Paul prayed that way. Even Jesus prayed, "Abba, Father, all things possible for you. Remove this cup from me. Yet not what I will, but what you will" (Mark 14:36), speaking of his impending death on the cross, where he would not only take on our sin but the full force of God's wrath.

You have probably heard that God has three answers to our prayers — yes, no, and not yet. Second Corinthians 12 adds a fourth, and what a powerful answer it is: "But he said to me, 'My grace is sufficient for you, for my power is made perfect in weakness'" (v. 9).

Paul knew about the sufficiency of God's undeserved kindness. In 2 Corinthians 4:8-10 Paul says that God in his grace kept him from being crushed when afflicted, kept him from despair, kept him from feeling forsaken, and protected him from destruction. What about God's grace regarding his thorn? In what way was God's grace sufficient for Paul's thorn in the flesh? Here's the answer: God's grace allowed Paul to press on in faith even though he had been daily harassed for fourteen years by this thorn, and even after praying and praying for God to take it away.

Many of us can relate to praying fervently for God to take our thorn away, to take us out of the storm. That prayer is perfectly understandable. But the question is, will you accept God's answer if he chooses not to deliver you, not to take the thorn away? Will you believe that the Lord's grace is sufficient for your storm, for whatever is harassing you?

To know that God's grace is sufficient, we need to remember whose grace it is. Verse 9 is a direct quotation of what Jesus told Paul, teaching us that the grace of God is found in Jesus Christ. The apostle John in his Gospel tells us in 1:14 that Jesus is "full of grace and truth", and "from his fullness we have all received, grace upon grace" (v. 16). Because the eternal Son of God has an eternal supply of grace, James can say that "he [continually] gives more grace" (4:6). The same grace that sustained Christ through the worst ordeal that any man or woman could ever face is available to you through him. Whatever your storm, God's grace is sufficient for it; and if your storm gets worse, "he gives more grace"!

The Power of Grace

Sometimes, though not always, the power of God's grace is seen in his deliverance. At the beginning of this second letter to the Corinthians, in 1:8-10, Paul talks about God's grace delivering him.

> *For we do not want you to be ignorant, brothers, of the affliction we experienced in Asia. For we were so utterly burdened beyond our strength that we despaired of life itself. Indeed, we felt that we had received the sentence of death. But that was to make us rely not on ourselves but on God who raises the dead. He delivered us from such a deadly peril, and he will deliver us. On him we have set our hope that he will deliver us again.*

His power shows itself in a remarkable way here. But sometimes God chooses not to deliver us, and then too he showers us with his grace. As Jesus says in chapter 12, "my power is made perfect in weakness." The power of the grace that Paul boasted in is God's power that enabled him to remain in the storm when his prayers for deliverance weren't answered. God's power was seen in Paul's weakness!

When we read that God's power is perfected in our weakness, this does not mean that God's power is deficient and needs perfecting. Rather, God's power is more clearly seen through our weakness.

So Paul's response and ours should be that we boast in our weaknesses. If one follows the word order in the original Greek in 12:9b it reads, "Gladly therefore I will boast in my weaknesses so that the power of Christ may rest upon me." The phrase "rest upon me" carries the idea of living in a tent. Christ's power camps over us. He has pitched his powerful presence over our lives.

So for the sake of Christ and his glory, Paul says in verse 10, he remains content in the storm. Whether he experiences weakness, insults, hardships, persecution, or calamities, he is "content." The word translated "content" is active, not passive. It could be translated "takes pleasure" or "delights in." Why would he delight in difficult circumstances? Because when he is weak, then he is strong.

Paul is rejoicing in the truth that because of his thorn he is weak, but his weakness is allowing God's power to be more clearly seen. Having been sucked dry by the storm, he delights in it, understanding that because of his thorn, God's power is not only resting on his life but is emanating from his life as well.

This remains true for God's children today. Many times I have seen someone go through a storm and thought, *I don't know how they're doing it.* Paul says in essence, "It's not me — it's God. It's his grace that is sustaining me, his grace that is supplying me with everything I need in body, mind, and soul to persevere through this." That is why Paul would say to Timothy in 2 Timothy 2:1, "You then, my child, be strengthened by the grace that is in Christ Jesus."

God's grace is sufficient and powerful. If you protest, "Man, I don't know if I can go any farther," God in his Word is saying, "I've got you covered. My grace is sufficient, and my power is being perfected in your weakness." Let his grace transform you to be more like Christ, and let Christ be seen through your weakness.

Scripture mentions four conduits from which Christ's powerful and sufficient grace overflows: his presence (the Holy Spirit), his Word, his people, and prayer.

HIS PRESENCE

The power and sufficiency of God's grace come from His presence mediated to us through His Spirit.

• "God is our refuge and strength, a very present help in trouble" (Psalm 46:1).

• "When you pass through the waters, I will be with you; and through the rivers, they shall not overwhelm you; when you walk through fire you shall not be burned, and the flame shall not consume you. . . . Fear not, for I am with you" (Isaiah 43:2, 5).

• "I will never leave you nor forsake you" (Hebrews 13:5; cf. Josh 1:5).

• "The Lord is near to the brokenhearted and saves the crushed in spirit" (Psalm 34:18).

• Jesus gave us the Holy Spirit, the Comforter who comes alongside us during our trials. The one who makes us alive sustains us spiritually.

• The Spirit intercedes for us. Romans 8:26 says, "The Spirit helps us in our weakness . . . the Spirit himself intercedes for us with groanings too deep for words." If you belong to God, you can be sure that the Spirit is interceding for you, praying that the Father would supply your every need.

• The Spirit gives us peace (Romans 8:6).

• God's power raised Christ from the dead, and his Spirit gives us power as we testify to him (Acts 1:3, 8).

• The Spirit guides us in truth, convicts us of sin, and assures us we belong to God (John 16:8, 13; Romans 8:16, 27), so that we don't shipwreck our faith.

• He makes us more like Christ — we are sanctified by the Spirit of God (1 Corinthians 6:11).

God's grace comes to us through his presence with us. Jesus is called Immanuel — "God with us." Before he left this earth, Christ said he would send his Spirit to reside in us. God mediates his presence through his Spirit, and the Holy Spirit's work really can't be separated from the second provision or conduit of grace — God's Word. God's Spirit works in tandem with God's Word.

HIS WORD

The power and sufficiency of God's grace also come to us through his Word.

• In Acts 20:32 Paul call God's Word "the word of his grace" .

• It sheds light on our path (Psalm 119:105). It helps us fight off temptation (Ephesians 6:17; cf. Jesus' example in this regard in Matthew 4:1-11).

• God's Word helps us fight the fight of faith, correcting feelings that can lead us to wrong conclusions about what is true concerning God and his character (see 2 Timothy 4:7).

• It reminds us of his promises.

• It tells us how to live in the storms — how we can worship in suffering, trust him in the storm, rejoice during trials, etc.

• It teaches, reproves, corrects, and trains us in righteousness, so that we are adequately equipped to do the good works that God created us to do (2 Timothy 3:16-17; cf. Ephesians 2:10).

• Along with the Word comes God's wisdom. God's wisdom is grace for us in the storm. James says that is exactly what we need. God's wisdom flows from his Word, is often received through his people, and is available to all who ask God for it. "If any of you lacks wisdom, let him ask God, who gives generously to all without reproach, and it will be given him" (James 1:5). His wisdom enables us to respond rightly to the trials we encounter.

HIS PEOPLE

Further, the power and sufficiency of God's grace come from his people. This happens:

• As other believers weep with us. We are called to weep with those who weep (Romans 12:15). That was the best thing Job's friends did. For the first seven days they wept for their friend, never saying a word (Job 2:11-13).

• As they share not only our sufferings, but the comfort they received when they experienced a storm (1 Corinthians 12:25; 2 Corinthians 1:3-7).

• As they pray for us. Paul told the Corinthian believers, "You also must help us by prayer" (2 Corinthians 1:11).

• As they give, meeting others' needs: "Now the full number of those who believed were of one heart and soul, and no one said that any of the things that belonged to him was his own, but they had everything in common. . . . There was not a needy person among them" (Acts 4:32, 34).

• As they hold up some of the weight of our burden. "Bear one another's burdens, and so fulfill the law of Christ" (Galatians 6:2).

I think it would be helpful for you to hear how Christian friends in our church cared for us. Neither my nor my wife's family live close by. So we really needed the help of our church family. Here are some of the ways God's grace flowed through his people to us.

First, I think of meals. I realize that most people aren't used to preparing food for seven people. Our neighbors were delighted as we brought leftovers to their house. I was grateful for the people who broke Lori's no dessert rule. We were given great meals — I'm still recovering.

I think of women coming over and grabbing a few baskets of laundry or the teams that would come over weekly to clean the house. Someone shoveled our driveway. My sister and her family did a Home & Garden Television (HGTV) "While You Were Out" bedroom project. Lori's chemo was rough, and the new look helped a lot. Friends came and planted flowers and cleaned up the yard and prepared the flowerbeds. One couple made lunches for two weeks when Lori had her second surgery. I will never forget when they walked through the door one Sunday night with boxes of supplies. Our kids were wowed by the treats, and we were overwhelmed at their kindness. Fifty lunches for two weeks. Every bag had a kid's name on it and a Scripture verse in it. Every bag had a note written to each of our children. I think of the special invites for the kids-cousins day at the Giesers. I remember a basket full of gifts for my wife, a quilt made by the women in our neighborhood complete with handwritten notes of encouragement, another quilt from our sister-in-law Cindy. There were notes and cards, most of them covered with Scripture. We treasured the visits of friends and family, and we rode on their prayers!

The sufficiency and power of God's grace poured out by our church family overwhelmed us. Paul speaks of this very thing when he says, "God, who comforts the downcast, comforted us by the coming of Titus" (1 Corinthians 7:6). In the same way, God comforted us by our friends' coming, by their sharing, by their love.

Some who are in the storm today are going through it alone because they haven't shared their storm with anyone else. If no one knows, no one can help shoulder the load. Trust God's family to be with you in your storm. You don't need to keep it to yourself or to hide it from caring friends. One of the gracious provisions God has given you — besides himself and his Word — is his people who will come with his Word and will in effect be Christ in the flesh to you, caring for you as his hands and his feet.

PRAYER

In addition, the power and sufficiency of God's grace come to us through prayer!

I have always believed in prayer, but having been the recipient of the prayers of God and his people, I can tell you that I believe James 5:16 more than ever: "The prayer of a righteous person has great power."

Remember this the next time you come alongside someone who's going through a storm. Don't ever think prayer is the least you can do. I believe it may be the *best* we can do for those in a storm.

There is no other way to explain the peace that Lori and I have experienced. Now, I want to be careful and not mislead anyone. Having God's peace doesn't mean there aren't any hard days — there are, but God's peace has been incredibly real and sustaining.

What gets us through is not our knowing the outcome of the storm — we don't. Rather it's the provision of God's grace through his abiding presence, his gracious Word, his loving people, and the power of prayer.

God brings storms into our lives for a reason. If you know Christ and you are going through a storm, you may feel like giving up. Hold on to God's grace, and remember that Jesus says to you, "My grace is sufficient for you!" If you don't know Christ as your personal Savior, he is allowing the storm that you are in so that you might discover his grace.

The Bible is clear. We come into a relationship with God only by his grace — his unmerited favor — through faith in Jesus Christ. Neither our faith nor our relationship with God are of our own doing. It is all a gift of God, not secured by our good works, but through Jesus' good work on the cross. All the glory goes to God. Receive God's grace.

Place your faith in Jesus, the one who died for you, and keep serving him!

Place your faith in Jesus, the one gives you his life.

Place your faith in Jesus, the one who gives his Helper, the Holy Spirit, to help you.

Place your faith in Jesus, the one who is coming for you.

Turn away from any self-sufficiency, and take hold of God's grace.

SCRIPTURES FOR REFLECTION

This is my comfort in my affliction, that your promise gives me life. . . . Before I was afflicted I went astray, but now I keep your word. . . . It is good for me that I was afflicted, that I might learn your statutes. . . . I know, O LORD, that your rules are righteous, and that in faithfulness you have afflicted me. . . . If your law had not been my delight, I would have perished in my affliction. (PSALM 119:50, 67, 71, 75, 92)

Have you not known? Have you not heard? The LORD is the everlasting God, the Creator of the ends of the earth. He does not faint or grow weary; his understanding is unsearchable. He gives power to the faint, and to him who has no might he increases strength. Even youths shall faint and be weary, and young men shall fall exhausted; but they who wait for the LORD shall renew their strength; they shall mount up with wings like eagles; they shall run and not be weary; they shall walk and not faint. (ISAIAH 40:28-31)

The Spirit himself bears witness with our spirit that we are children of God, and if children, then heirs — heirs of God and fellow heirs with Christ, provided we suffer with him in order that we may also be glorified with him. For I consider that the sufferings of this present time are not worth comparing with the glory that is to be revealed to us. (ROMANS 8:16-18)

Blessed be the God and Father of our Lord Jesus Christ, the Father of mercies and God of all comfort, who comforts us in all our affliction, so that we may be able to comfort those who are in any affliction, with the comfort with which we ourselves are comforted by God. For as we share abundantly in Christ's sufferings, so through Christ we share abundantly in comfort too. If we are afflicted, it is for your comfort and salvation; and if we are comforted, it is for your comfort, which you experience when you patiently endure the same sufferings that we suffer. Our hope for you is unshaken, for we know that as you share in our sufferings, you will also share in our comfort. For we do not want you to be ignorant, brothers, of the affliction we experienced in Asia. For we were so utterly burdened beyond our strength that we despaired of life itself. Indeed, we felt that we had received the sentence of death. But that was to make us rely not on ourselves but on God who raises the dead. He delivered us from such a deadly peril, and he will deliver us. On him we have set our hope that he will deliver us again. You also must help us by prayer, so that many will give thanks on our behalf for the blessing granted us through the prayers of many.

2 CORINTHIANS 1:3-11, ESV

5

GOD'S GRACE
THROUGH THE STORMS

The storms of life blow into our lives unannounced. Some graciously leave as quickly as they came. But others seemingly never move, hovering over us, pummeling us every day, and we wonder when the dark clouds will lift, when will they rid themselves of their fury.

Two years ago (at the time of this writing), my family entered a storm — lightning struck out of a clear blue sky. My wife found out she had breast cancer, and her cancer had spread to her lymph nodes. Four surgeries later, with chemotherapy and radiation now in our rearview mirror, we are glad to hear my wife use the words "a year ago"! Although the doctors are quick to use the phrase "cancer-free," we know they can't put it writing. So we continue to trust God, thanking him for every day.

Last January my dad had quintuple bypass surgery the day after Lori's mastectomy. Two weeks after surgery he almost bled to death. On May 9 of last year my healthy mother unexpectedly died of a heart attack. As a pastor I realize that most people in my church have gone through or are going through a storm. But not all storms are alike. Some storms are like spring showers, others like a tornado that carves a path of destruction a mile wide and ten miles long.

Here is a quick reminder of where we have been as we have considered the storms of life and God's part in them.

Chapter One: God of the Storms. Job 1 teaches us that God is Lord over our storms, sovereignly in control of that which appears to be completely out of control. He not only allows them to come, but he in fact brings them to his own. Our world completely changes in those storms, but our God is the same, allowing us through tears and with great anguish to worship him even in the eye of the storm.

Chapter Two: God with Us. Psalm 46 reminds us that God is with us in the storm; he is not hovering off in the distance, detached or distracted. He is a very present help in trouble; he is our refuge and strength. Therefore we can trust him in the storms of life.

Chapter Three: God's Purposes for the Storms. Hebrews 12:3-11 reminds us of two of God's purposes for our trials. First, storms draw us to Christ; and second, storms make us more like Christ. As a result we can rejoice and thank God for the good work that he is doing in our lives through the storms. By God's grace the worst days of our life can be good days. By God's grace the words *hard* and *good* can both be used to describe our storms.

Chapter Four: The God Who Provides. We see from 2 Corinthians 12:7-10 that God's grace is both sufficient and powerful for each and every storm, so that through his gracious provisions of his Spirit, his Word, his people, and prayer we are able to endure the storms, fighting the good fight of faith, all to the glory of God.

Grace through the storms is a powerful truth that will greatly encourage those who are going through such times right now. Second Corinthians 1:3-11 tells us that God's grace doesn't just meet us in the storm — his grace actually flows through us to others even while we are in the tempest. The very people who are suffering receive God's comfort and are equipped to share his comfort with others. God's grace begins to flow even from the eye of the storm and continues to flow over the years.

We have all known people who have strengthened us through their storm. My friends Dawid and Zelna came to Wheaton, Illinois, from South Africa. They had recently been married back home and found their way into the life of our church. Dawid was a rugby player, a big strong man. Yet the strength that I will always remember was his strong faith in Christ and his gentle and kind spirit. Right before they were married Dawid noticed some stiffness in his neck. Tests revealed that it was a cancerous tumor lodged in his spinal chord. Throughout their short married life Dawid struggled with cancer. There were countless surgeries (some lasting over sixteen hours!) — several on his neck to remove tumors, surgeries on his chest, surgeries on his shoulders. There were endless treatments of chemotherapy and radiation.

Because the tumors had lodged in his vertebrae, they had to be removed. The doctors inserted titanium rods and plates in order to support Dawid's head. Five months after one of his many surgeries, the doctors found that one of his metal plates had actually pierced his esophagus, explaining his constant sore throat, his problems with bleeding, and his everyday battle to get food down without coughing and choking, resulting in the loss of fifty pounds. In my more than twenty years as a pastor, I have never seen a storm hover like Dawid and Zelna's. But through it all they pointed me to Christ as they patiently endured suffering. Their e-mails read like epistles — they were honest but always filled with praise. They constantly thanked their friends for their prayers, and there was no doubt that their hope was firmly resting on God. My visits with them had a similar pattern. I would go to encourage them and would always leave humbled and strengthened by the flow of grace that filled my soul. Dawid and Zelna and their young son David returned to South Africa last year for what they thought would be a short visit. Dawid died shortly after arriving. God's comfort continues to surround

Zelna, and by God's grace it will continue to flow through her in the years to come.

God comforts us in all our afflictions so that we may be able to comfort those in affliction with the comfort we ourselves have received from God. God's grace through the storms!

When Paul talks about his experience of God's comfort we note two reflexes. The first reflex is the reflex of praise—he thanks God for being the God of all comfort who comforts us in all our affliction (vv. 3-4a). The second reflex is sharing—he shares the comfort he has received with others who are hurting (vv. 4-11).

THE REFLEX OF PRAISING GOD
(VV. 3-4A)

"Blessed be the God and Father of our Lord Jesus Christ, the Father of mercies and God of all comfort." Who is this God? None other than the Father of our Lord Jesus Christ, the one whose suffering is beyond compare, the Father who comforted his Son all the way to the cross, all the way to death and beyond.

Who is this God? He is "the Father of mercies." When God revealed his glory to Moses and showed him his goodness, "The LORD passed before him and proclaimed, 'The LORD, the LORD, a God merciful and gracious, slow to anger, and abounding in steadfast love and faithfulness'" (Exodus 34:6). That is who God is — "the Father of all mercies"! His mercy — his goodness — meets us in our misery. That is why the psalmist cries out, "Be merciful to me, O God, be merciful to me, for in you my soul takes refuge; in the shadow of your wings I will take refuge, till the storms of destruction pass by" (Psalm 57:1).

Who is this God? He is "the . . . God of all comfort, who comforts us in all our affliction" (2 Corinthians 1:3-4). "All comfort" in all kinds of affliction is ours through "the . . . God of all comfort." That means there isn't a storm in which we can't find God's comfort. It also means we will never experience God's comfort apart from going through a storm. No affliction, no divine comfort. My children have known our comfort through their own pain; as children it was their cuts and bruises that introduced them to my comfort.

This past fall I was with our youngest son Luke on a Wednesday night for a dad and boys program called Treeclimbers. One of the favorite games is sharks and minnows. Luke is our six-year-old redhead whose freckled face usually sports a sweet smile. The two sharks called the boys over, and the mad dash began. As I made my way across the floor, my eye noticed that one of the boys fell — toppled is a better word. It was Luke. He stepped on a loose shoelace and hit the floor face first. By the time I got there, his taut body and clenched hands and jaw let me know he was seizing. My heart was racing and aching for my hurting child. His injury released a flood of affection and tender care. I remember praying, *Lord, I can't take another crisis — please help.*

After he started to come to, I picked him up in my arms and carried him down four flights of stairs to wait for the paramedics. The next four hours were spent at the emergency room with his mom and dad at his side as his four siblings waited at home, concerned about their little brother. Thanks to God's kindness, Luke's fall was the entrée to more comfort. Remember, no affliction, no divine comfort. There is grace through the storm because he is "the . . . God of all comfort, who comforts us in all our affliction." Praise God for the comfort that comes to us!

It is important that our definition for *comfort* not be too narrow. If it is, our expectations regarding God's comfort could leave us disappointed and at the same time mislead us as we seek to comfort others. Some people hear *comfort*, and they immediately assume that God's comfort makes us feel better. God's comfort certainly consoles us in our affliction, but verse 6 makes it clear that God's comfort also helps us and strengthens us to patiently endure suffering: "If we are afflicted, it is for your comfort and salvation; and if we are comforted, it is for your comfort, which you experience when you patiently endure the same sufferings that we suffer." God's comfort strengthens us and helps us and encourages us to continue to trust God and to worship him even in the storm. Verse 4 reminds us that God's comfort comes *in* our affliction, not after it!

The Greek word used here means "comfort, console, encourage, or help." It is the same root word used for the Holy Spirit when Jesus calls him "the Helper" (John 14:16, 26). The root of that word shows up ten times in these nine verses in 2 Corinthians 1.

God's comfort, then, is more than a good feeling we receive after we have suffered. It is strength given during the storm, enabling us to patiently endure even more! This is exactly how Paul ministered to the early believers.

> *When they had preached the gospel to that city and had made many disciples, they returned to Lystra and to Iconium and to Antioch, strengthening the souls of the disciples, encouraging [the same root word for "comfort"] them to continue in the faith, and saying that through many tribulations we must enter the kingdom of God. (Acts 14:21-22)*

Do you feel like giving up in your storm? Are you thinking about discarding your faith? In the storms of life we all desperately need God's mercy and comfort. Praise God for his comfort that comes to us!

THE REFLEX OF COMFORTING OTHERS
(VV. 4B-11)

Here is what we know from 2 Corinthians 1. If we never suffer, we will never experience God's comfort. We know that the God of all comfort is able to comfort us in all our afflictions, all our troubles, all our hard circumstances. We know that God's grace comes to us in the storms. But now Paul is going to go further and tell us that suffering prepares us and qualifies us to comfort others. That is what the "so that" is about in verse 4: "who comforts us in all our affliction, so that we may be able to comfort those who are in any affliction, with the comfort with which we ourselves are comforted by God." The comfort that comes to us in all our affliction becomes the comfort that we can share in any affliction. Verse 5 and following tells us how this works.

Verse 5 says, "For as we share abundantly in Christ's sufferings, so through Christ we share abundantly in comfort too." Abundant suffering leads to abundant comfort — comfort that will not only meet your need but will go on to meet the needs of others. God's eternal supply of comfort meets us, fills us, and then flows through us as we share it with others. Because God's comfort is abundant, there's plenty to go around.

Two weeks before Lori was diagnosed with breast cancer, our friend Diane shared about God's sustaining grace in her life over the past year. She did this at our church's Thanksgiving service, where people are given an opportunity to express their thanks to God. As we recounted the testimonies that night, Lori and I both agreed that Diane's was the highlight. For the last year Diane had been battling ovarian cancer. She shared how God's comfort had come to her through his Word. Her words of praise to God in the midst of the storm encouraged us. Little did we know what was around our corner.

Verse 6 tells us that God's comfort flowing through us is part of God's plan: "If we are afflicted, it is for your comfort and salvation; and if we are comforted, it is for your comfort, which you experience when you patiently endure the same sufferings that we suffer."

Our suffering is corporate in nature, not individualistic. Your suffering is not just about you — it's about others too, and not just those close to you, but even others you may not even know. There is a saying in Africa that speaks to this very point: "I am because we are, and because we are I am."

When we go through suffering, we can feel very lonely. Truly no one but God knows what we are going through. Listen to the litany of woe Paul gives us in 2 Corinthians 11:24 and following:

Five times I received at the hands of the Jews the forty lashes less one. Three times I was beaten with rods. Once I was stoned. Three times I was shipwrecked; a night and a day I was adrift at sea; on frequent journeys, in danger from rivers, danger from rob-bers, danger from my own people, danger from Gentiles, danger in the city, danger in the wilderness, danger at sea, danger from false brothers; in toil and hardship, through many a sleepless night, in hunger and thirst, often without food, in cold and expo-sure. And, apart from other things, there is the daily pressure on me of my anxiety for all the churches. (vv. 24-28)

Verse 6 is an important reminder that it's not just about us — it's about all of us — all of God's people. That means Paul understood that as personal as his beatings were, as severe his dangers, his suf-ferings weren't just about himself. That is clearly seen in his letter to his friends in Philippi.

I want you to know, brothers, that what has happened to me has really served to advance the gospel, so that it has become known throughout the whole imperial guard and to all the rest that my imprisonment is for Christ. And most of the brothers, having become confident in the Lord by my imprisonment, are much more bold to speak the word without fear. (Philippians 1:12-14)

Paul was the one in prison, but he understood how God was using his imprisonment to strengthen and embolden his brothers and sisters in Christ to speak the Word (the gospel) without fear.

Suffering is corporate because of our unity in Christ. We are brothers and sisters in his family and members together of his one body. That is why, "if one member suffers, all suffer together" (1 Corinthians 12:26). When you are going through suffering, you might feel all alone; but don't let those feelings dupe you into thinking that it's about you alone.

Sometimes we feel all alone because we decide not to tell others about our storm — we decide to go it alone. For others in the body to give you comfort, they need to know that you need comfort. Don't let pride or anything else keep you from sharing your need. Some people think others have it much worse; others cringe to be in the spotlight; still others think they can make it on their own ("besides, everyone is so busy"). The bottom line is, very few people wake up in the morning and say, "I can't wait to ask someone for help today." We pride ourselves on being independent and self-reliant, but it is the gift of receiving that makes sharing possible. The flow of grace stops when the need for grace is not raised. God's plan is for grace to come to us from him and to flow through us to those in need for his glory. Exercise the gift of receiving when you are in the storm! Are you going through it alone?

Paul is convinced that his friends at Corinth will share in God's comfort. Verses 7-10 tell us why. "Our hope for you is unshaken, for we know that as you share in our sufferings, you will also share in our comfort" (v. 7). Paul's confidence is rooted in his experience. Verses 8-10 tell us about a time in Asia when he was delivered by God from an awful situation: "For we do not want you to be ignorant, brothers, of the affliction we experienced in Asia. For we were so utterly burdened beyond our strength that we despaired of life itself. Indeed, we felt that we had received the sentence of death. But that was to make us rely not on ourselves but on God who raises the dead. He delivered us from such a deadly peril, and he will deliver us. On him we have set our hope that he will deliver us again."

The historical setting, debated by scholars, is not important. If it was, God would have recorded it for us. What's important are the three truths Paul wanted them (and us) to know.

God uses storms to show us our need (v. 9). God brings suffering into our lives to keep us from self-reliance. Like a hurricane, storms tear down our self-sufficiency. They force us to grow in greater dependence upon God. And our dependence on God reveals more of his greatness!

God uses storms to demonstrate his power and faithfulness (v. 10). God has delivered, and he will deliver us, and he will deliver us again! God's rescue and provision in the past becomes the basis for our hope in a future deliverance. The worst thing that can happen in suffering is to lose hope. If you are a Christian, you have experienced God's deliverance. The Bible is full of accounts of God delivering his people through and from all kinds of troubles. God's past acts of liberation fill us with hope as we deal with the present and look into the future.

Let's keep in mind that God's rescue comes in several ways. First, there is deliverance *from* affliction — when God graciously pulls you out of your difficulty. Second, there is deliverance *in* affliction. This is the help and encouragement that allows us to patiently endure our suffering. Third, there is the ultimate deliverance that comes through death (cf. 2 Corinthians 5:1, 4b).

God uses our prayers to strengthen and deliver those who are suffering (v. 11): "You also must help us by prayer, so that many will give thanks on our behalf for the blessing granted us through the prayers of many."

Zelna wrote, "Thank you for your thoughts and prayers. We desperately need them, and we so appreciate them. . . . Our sadness and worry changes to courage and hope through your prayers and support. . . . We honestly believe that all the prayers that are prayed for Dawid and us lie firmly on God's heart and that he truly listens. Thank you."

Paul's unshaken hope for those who follow Christ and are suffering is that God will deliver them, and he understands the vital role of prayer as part of God's rescue. The result of saints' prayers will be deliverance that leads to thanksgiving and praise to God. Paul says the same thing in Philippians 1:19, "for I know that through your prayers and the help of the Spirit of Jesus Christ this will turn out for my deliverance."

Yes, God wants us to worship him in the storm. Yes, God wants us to trust him, for he is our refuge and strength. Yes, God wants our storms to drive us to Christ and make us more like him. Yes, God wants us to experience his powerful and sufficient grace that comes through his Spirit, through the Word, through God's people, and through prayer. But God also wants us to know that his grace comes in abundance and flows through us as we patiently endure suffering. The comfort we receive from God becomes the comfort we share. Apart from suffering we would never know God's comfort and would never be indebted to his mercy or equipped to share his gracious comfort.

This truth came crashing home on October 14, 1992. Earlier that year our family, including our three young girls, had spent a six-month sabbatical in Switzerland. Lori's pregnancies were very traumatic. She usually ended up in the hospital. In fact, after the first pregnancy I diplomatically removed myself from all "family planning" decisions. While away, we prayed for God's direction concerning a fourth child. He answered. We left Switzerland with Lori pregnant and sick. Within a few weeks of our return, Lori was hospitalized for several weeks as the doctors tried to stabilize both her and the baby. Lori's sickness continued another ten weeks. Most of that time she was hydrated and nourished intravenously.

We were in survival mode — three kids under seven, no family in town, ministry responsibilities at church. And on top of that I had the bright idea of getting a Labrador pup to replace our yellow Lab that had died while we were on sabbatical! Lori was miserable and suffering tremendously — she literally couldn't even keep a sip of water down. And then one day, seemingly out of nowhere, came a miracle! Lori felt great and wanted to join us for dinner — deep-dish pizza! I couldn't believe it — from not being able to swallow water to eating deep-dish pizza! God is good — the storm had finally lifted.

What I didn't know was that Lori was afraid she had lost the baby. The next week Lori had a scheduled doctor's visit, and providentially I went along. The doctor slipped on his stethoscope and started to listen. He moved here and there, searching, I guessed, for the heartbeat. I still didn't know anything was wrong until I noticed Lori's leg starting to shake. And when she began to cry, it all began to sink in! "I can't find a heartbeat," the doctor said with concern. "You need an ultrasound." Later that afternoon the doctor confirmed our worst fears: Our baby had died.

We were instructed to go to the hospital and check into Labor and Delivery. Our room was just around the corner from where Claire had been born a little less than two years before. Lori was induced, and a few hours later delivered a beautiful baby boy, some five months along in gestation. Gabriel was perfect. We cried as we held him. He was so small that he fit in the palm of my hand. His feet were as long as my thumbnail. I remembered the words that my pastor and friend Kent Hughes had shared many times: "Hold the things that God gives you with an open hand, understanding that they are gifts from God, understanding that the harder we grip them, the harder it will be when they are taken from us." That is how we held all our children, and now God was doing what we knew he had a right to do. And so with an open hand we handed our baby boy to the nurse and gave him back to the Lord, entrusting his soul into his merciful care.

As we left the hospital they rolled Lori to the back door where I would pick her up. Would you believe that the woman seated next to her was holding twins. The ride home from the hospital with a newborn baby in the backseat is almost as great as the day of his or her birth, but going home from the hospital with no one in the backseat is excruciating. A few weeks later our five-year-old wrote a letter to Gabriel:

Dear Gabriel,

I hope you have a good time in heaven. This is Bridget who is talking. I wish you could be in a safe spot. When we are in heaven we will get to know you. When we are in heaven can we play with each other? I hope you noticed us. I like to remember my brother and sisters. That's all for now. Good-bye.

Love, Bridget

Some friends from church, Niel and Kathleen Nielson, came over as soon as they heard. Their comfort was tender and strong. They too had lost a son, some two months before, at just about the same point as in Kathleen's pregnancy. They knew our pain, and they shared the comfort that they received and were receiving from God. *Comforted to comfort — grace through the storms.*

It shouldn't surprise us when God grants us opportunities to share the comfort we have received from him in our storm with brothers and sisters who are going through their storm. Since losing our baby Gabriel, several couples have gone through a similar trial, and we have been able to encourage and strengthen and console them, using the comfort that God brought into our lives.

If you are in a storm or have just come out of one, remember that the God of all comfort will comfort you in your storm and will use you to strengthen and encourage others both as you endure suffering and as you share the abundant comfort that you have received and are receiving from God. Praise God for his grace that comes to us. Praise God for his grace that flows through us.

God is glorified when sufferers worship him and trust him and allow the force of the storm to drive them to Christ and to make them like Christ. God is glorified as people take hold of his all-sufficient grace. Grace through the storm as we receive God's comfort. Grace through the storm as we allow others to minister God's comfort to us. Grace through the storm as we strengthen others by patiently enduring suffering. Grace through the storm as we share the comfort we have received from God.

Blessed be the God and Father of our Lord Jesus Christ, the Father of mercies and God of all comfort, who comforts us in all our affliction, so that we may be able to comfort those who are in any affliction, with the comfort with which we ourselves are comforted by God. (2 Corinthians 1:3-4)

SCRIPTURES FOR REFLECTION

Now may our Lord Jesus Christ himself, and God our Father, who loved us and gave us eternal comfort and good hope through grace, comfort your hearts and establish them in every good work and word. (2 THESSALONIANS 2:16-17)

Many are the afflictions of the righteous, but the LORD delivers him out of them all. (PSALM 34:19)

We rejoice in our sufferings, knowing that suffering produces endurance, and endurance produces character, and character produces hope, and hope does not put us to shame, because God's love has been poured into our hearts through the Holy Spirit who has been given to us. (ROMANS 5:3-5)

Appendix:
Testimonies of
Fellow Pilgrims

On the following pages you will find words of encouragement and comfort from friends who weathered storms in their marriage, family, health, employment, and even the death of a loved one. I hope their words followed by a few choice quotations will encourage your heart.

Marriage

The storm in my soul began when I found out that the foundation of my marriage was built on falsehood. My husband, whom I thought was a devout believer, who spent time in God's Word and ministry in the church, had been leading a "double life" for our entire 15-year marriage. This double life was largely carried out while he traveled weekly for his job. This secret life included alcohol addiction, pornography addiction, and serial extramarital affairs. My heart was broken. As I began to grieve the deceit and betrayal in our marriage, I questioned God's sovereignty. How could He know and "watch" my husband's choices and not have intervened or let me know somehow.

I genuinely loved God, and had tried to serve Him with my life, tell others of His saving grace—and this was what He allowed for me and my children? I felt God was disloyal to my dedication and love for Him. Maybe I had done something wrong, or wasn't "good" enough? In His grace, God continually drew me to His Word, and comforted me with the knowledge of who He was and of His trustworthiness. Through His Word, and the care of other believers, God assured me of His love, care, and goodness. It wasn't God that was unfaithful, but only my husband. The fact that God HAD seen now gave me comfort rather than a sense of betrayal. He had protected and cared for me and my children in countless ways, because He was watching.

A friend gave me Psalm 33 early on, and it gave me such comfort, particularly verse 4, "For the Word of the Lord is right and true; he is faithful in all he does." Also v. 18, "The eyes of the Lord are on those who fear him, and those whose hope is in his unfailing love . . . he is our help and shield."

Being an avid reader, I read at least 30 books during this time about all the problems I was dealing with, most written by Christian authors. Many were helpful, but none gave me the comfort and wisdom I needed like God's Word, found in the Scriptures: Seek godly counsel. Trust in God. He is working out His purposes for your good and His glory (Ephesians 1:11).

Several key lessons learned through our marital storm:

• Daily seek to do whatever God tells you to do. Pray for guidance and keep reading the Bible (even when you have trouble focusing). Trust the Holy Spirit to counsel you and lead you in truth. He will.

• Your obedience to God is not a *guarantee* of a restored marriage, but it will guarantee that your life will be safe and secure in Christ. We must never obey God to "put Him under obligation" to do something for us. Obey Him because it is right and wise to do so.

• When you experience the raging river of anguish, doubt, questions, and fear, stay within the banks of God's sovereignty *and* God's goodness. Don't allow your search for answers to cross those banks.

• Throughout your storm, look for God's kindnesses to you. In faith expect them, and learn to recognize them. Be thankful that God is with you, providing for you in the storm.

• Physical weakness and human brokenness can coexist with faith. Don't assume that your faith is immobilized when your mind and body are.

For it is not an enemy who reproaches me,
Then I could bear it:
Nor is it one who hates me,
who has exalted himself against me,
Then I could hide myself from him.
But it is you, a man my equal,
My companion and my familiar friend.
We who had sweet fellowship together,
walked in the house of God in the throng.

PSALM 55:12-14

How can one ever truly prepare for the storm of marital infidelity?

One thing I do know. No matter what the form of our particular storm, the calm through it will only come from our already cultivated relationship with the Lord. I don't think I learned any great new truths, but it was my already solid base of faith in God and His Word that sustained me during the storm. How thankful I am that I had cultivated my walk with the Lord before my storm. Not to be discounted is the blessing of true friends that came alongside me. I must add that it is often surprising to see who our true friends really are at a time like this!

How wonderful to be able to write this now, fourteen years later, and tell you that the Lord enabled me to stay in my marriage and experience the reconciliation that only He can bring. One of the closing verses of the already quoted Psalm says, "Cast your burden upon the Lord, and He will sustain you: He will never allow the righteous to be shaken."

RELATIONSHIPS/FAMILY

God's Word remains comforting and challenging in times of great distress. When faced with the unwanted reality of becoming a single parent, I learned that the Lord comforts us so that we can comfort those with the same comfort we have received (2 Corinthians 1:3-5). At the same time, the God of comfort reminded me that I was to love my enemies (Matthew 5:43). This meant loving my ex-spouse and anyone who mistreated me because of my situation. It meant teaching the wounded child to love as well. As we learned to love, God's comfort deepened. I believe that we would not have had God's comfort for long if we had failed to move, however haltingly, toward full obedience in love. Pain is an opportunity to learn the depths of love, as well as a time to be comforted.

Ten years had gone by. Ten years since our oldest son had walked out on his wife, threw out God whom he had served diligently, and told us, his parents and brothers and sisters, to get lost. The hurt was so deep we rarely talked about it. Occasionally at Christmas or a family wedding someone would murmur, "Wish Chuck was here."

Perversely the hurt we had in common bonded the rest of us. The family had doubled in size, and little nieces and nephews prayed for Uncle Chuck whom they had never seen to come back to the family and love God again.

Once when several of our married children were together at our house, they prayed earnestly for their lost brother. The very next morning we told them that at a dinner the night before, the mother of one of Chuck's high school classmates reported that her son had crossed paths with Chuck. He was a college professor teaching English!

Following that lead another son and his wife flew across several states to find him in person. They spent a somewhat tense but mutually satisfying weekend together. Our hopes shot up. But shortly after that Chuck closed the door again and barred it against all communication with the family. Year after year went by, another thirteen years. The family more than doubled in size again. Our faith was stretched.

Then with no announcement Chuck showed up at his brother's door. He could no longer keep his twenty-one-year-old daughter in the dark about his family — her family too — a big family about which she knew almost nothing. But before he could bring her into the family, he had to come himself. Tentatively. Twenty-three years of silence couldn't be tossed away like a used paper plate. "But love and I had the wit to win; we drew a circle that took him in." God is the author of all love.

HEALTH/DEATH

When our beloved daughter was too depressed to function and too confused to let anyone help her, we were in great anguish. At that time I found great comfort in all kinds of beauty. The beauties of nature, music, the familiar cadences of the Psalms, and the blessed order and truth of church services (even when I was too sorrowful and overwhelmed to absorb much from sermons) sustained me, comforted me, and helped me hold onto my belief that the God who created such beauty is indeed good and the sustainer of what he creates. Because the things I've listed touch the emotions, somehow they helped me *feel* the connection to my heavenly Father which I so desperately needed.

The other thing that helped me was this question and answer from the Heidelberg Catechism, which dates back to 1563. "Q. What is your only comfort in life and death? A. That I, with body and soul, both in life and death, am not my own, but belong unto my faithful Savior Jesus Christ." I find this eloquent statement bracing and reorienting. It challenges my temptation to find security in anything but the Lord, and my place, and that of my loved ones, in anything but his perfect will. My serenity is not in a particular hoped-for outcome but in my Savior himself.

So, do you ever get mad at God?

Why do people ask me? Why should I even think of being mad?

First of all, being mad is not my nature. Secondly, being mad at God is a total anomaly. That's like hating chocolate or ice cream.

Sure, I get frustrated that I am disabled now. I cannot do the things that I have spent my lifetime (over half a century) preparing for and doing — holding a book or a newspaper, using a bar of soap, a glass of water . . .

OK, so I still have my head (even though that is where my injury occurred). I can think and speak (all relearned) and act like a normal person (to most people outside my family). But, most significantly, not being able to do the "hands-on" parts of my professional career is a continual challenge.

Do I ever get mad at God?

How can I when Scripture reminds me: "I know the plans I have for you . . . plans to give you hope [peace] and a future" (Jeremiah 29:11).

My pastor always tells me, "God is sovereign and He is good." As I think about that it makes me go to my knees in humility. How can I come up swinging?

God's plans are settled. They are eternal. I may not know what they are, but He does. I can rest in that and have new beginnings.
Additional Scripture:
"Casting all your care upon Him because He cares for you."
"My God shall supply all your needs . . ."
"Cast your burdens upon the Lord and He will sustain you."

"In the year that King Uzziah died, I saw the Lord." When our college-age son died we saw the Lord like never before, experiencing his mercy, grace and comfort. Look for God in your loss.

Being diagnosed with cancer at a young age is a unique gift from the Lord. It has forced me to learn and accept His plan for my life and not be discontent with life. It has taught me each day is a gift regardless of what it brings. The Lord has shown Himself to be merciful in this season of my life. Psalm 34:4 says, "I sought the Lord and He answered me and delivered me from all my fears."

Two verses became lifelines for my husband and me during my husband's six-month struggle with cancer before his death.

My times are in your hands; deliver me from my enemies and from those who pursue me. (Psalm 31:15)

As for God, his way is perfect; the Word of the LORD is flawless. He is a shield for all who take refuge in him. (Psalm 18:30)

These promises from God, which had always been comforting, sustained our spiritual lives during those months as we clung to them. The promises, of course, had not changed, but our circumstances had. From having healthy bodies, a loving marriage, and fulfilling ministry, our lives plunged overnight into the reality of ravaging, terminal cancer. But as my husband's body wasted away, his spirit shone even more brightly — a mystery only possible because of the life of Christ in him.

We discovered that God's promises are true either all the time or none of the time. They are true in the joyful and the sorrowful times. We discovered also in a deepened way that God's promises are true not only through the sorrows of this life but for eternity. And it is eternity that is the greater reality. As C. S. Lewis says in *Mere Christianity*, "Christianity asserts that every individual human being is going to live forever, and this must be either true or false. . . . If individuals live only seventy years, then a state or nation, or a civilization, which may last for a thousand years, is more important than an individual. But if Christianity is true, then the individual is not only more important but incomparably more important, for he is everlasting and the life of a state or a civilization, compared with his, is only a moment."

Miracles: When our deathly ill two-year-old daughter lapsed into a coma and ran a temperature of 107 degrees, we prayed that God would spare her life. Those prayers were answered, and then we prayed that there would be no permanent damage and that her recovery would be complete. Again prayers were answered, and we knew that we had experienced the wonderful miracle of healing.

A few years later our son, our youngest child, was diagnosed with serious brain damage, and again we looked to God for another miracle. This time, however, there was no healing, and our prayers took a new direction as we asked God to give us the wisdom, ability, and help to cope with a constantly challenging family situation. For over forty years God has been faithful by sending into our life countless caring individuals who have been meaningfully involved with our son and who have allowed us to enjoy the equally wonderful miracle of coping.

Cold-blooded murder: Was my seventy-five-year-old sister a Christian martyr in California? Her pastor in his funeral eulogy declared she was as she was working in a Christian institution when she was brutally killed with blows on her head by a handyman who coveted her car. To get the keys from her purse, he had to get rid of her. Hopefully she suffered only briefly before seeing her Savior face to face.

The ministrations of her fellow church members in our time of grief will never be forgotten. After three days of tears and sharing memories of our sister, mother, and grandmother, we saw God's rainbow in the sky — a rare sight in that part of California. We took it as a sign that God was in covenant with us. Not just a covenant that there would never be another universal flood, but a sign that he was watching over *us*, that he would never leave *us*.

The summer of 1996 found me a happy young mom of a busy toddler. Life couldn't get much better. I had hung up my career about a year earlier to pursue my dream job: stay-at-home mom. We knew we'd better get started on Child #2 since Child #1 took three years to arrive. We were very excited when we got pregnant right away. But within a week of learning the good news, things started to get difficult. I became very sick. By the time I was six weeks pregnant I was hospitalized.

Soon I couldn't keep down a sip of water, so I had to be fed intravenously. I was throwing up forty times a day and was so weak, I couldn't be left alone. People came in shifts to stay with my son and me while my husband worked.

Everything I based my identity on seemed to be stripped away.

Wife? Now I was just someone for my husband to hook I.V.'s to every morning. As a mother, I didn't have the strength to lift my son. A friend? I felt more like a burden than a friend to those who came to help out. Homemaker? No way. Even my body and my health were taken. My illness caused my gall bladder to shut down, and I underwent surgery in November.

I felt like the only things I had to hold on to were God and the baby I carried.

On December 3 the doctor was unable to locate the baby's heartbeat. An ultrasound confirmed that the baby had died, and I was admitted to the hospital to deliver our perfectly formed, eighteen-week-old-boy.

Of course, my health quickly improved, and I was once again able to be the wife, mother, and friend that I so wanted to be. But God showed me a glimpse of what it would be like if all I had and held dear were taken from me. If I lost everything, I would have God. And I know that He is enough. All those months of suffering may have seemed like a waste; I didn't get the privilege of raising my son. But I did gain the privilege of knowing the sufficiency of God's love. God *is* enough.

On a very hot summer day, our eleven-year-old son suddenly and mysteriously lost his memory for all people, places, and events. Numerous medical and psychological tests, counseling, visits to a large assortment of physicians and therapists, including the major medical centers in Chicago and the Mayo Clinic, turned up nothing. To top it off, he would inexplicably pass out whenever his body temperature reached approximately 98.6 or during any sort of exercise. It was frightening, baffling, and wearing on the whole family. Although my husband and I are in the medical field, I found that we were fairly well dismissed by nearly every physician we encountered when Tim's symptoms and the results of his tests didn't fit into their experiential grid.

The only way we survived our ordeal was through the love and support of our church family. Week after week, members of our life group and members of our Sunday school class would pray for him. They asked us how we were doing. They offered advice and consolation. The outpouring of love was amazing. I don't think we can understand how much God loves us — and how much he demonstrates his love through the caring of his people — until we go through some type of trauma like this. Whether or not you are going through storms, get involved in your church family; particularly a small life group that loves, sustains, and supports you.

One Sunday, ten months later, Tim's memory returned as suddenly and inexplicably as it had disappeared — in the church service — on Mother's Day.

It was through the death of our infant son that we came to wrestle with the sovereignty of God and ultimately find a deeper walk with God than we ever could have imagined. When life throws you into a storm like burying your firstborn infant child, you are shaken to the core of your being. The blessing in that is, it is then that we approach God and His sovereignty from a rare perspective. We come to Him stripped of all pride, broken, desperately aware of our hopelessness apart from Christ. It is in our weakness that we find His strength, hope, comfort, and salvation.

Our advice to you who are in the midst of the storm of death is to cling to Christ. You do this crying out to the Lord with your needs, your fears, your doubts and pain. He hears the cries of His people and promises to comfort those who mourn. God is close to the brokenhearted! During this storm read the Word; bathe yourself daily in His Word. Let Scripture wash over you like rain in the storm, for in it you will find hope, healing, and comfort; in it you will find Christ! He will walk with you in the storm, and as you cling to Him, you will find your faith stronger once you have weathered the storm. You will find that life, God, His Word, His Church, and the hope of heaven were never so precious as they are to you now. Godspeed to each of you who are weathering the storm of death. May it lead you home, to the Savior!

My storm began with the birth of my son. At birth we realized that all was not normal with him, and as time went on, more and more "abnormalities" were discovered. Before we knew it, we were thrown into life with a disabled child. Soon my life was consumed with this disability — doctors, therapies, special equipment, surgeries. I felt as if I was drowning in all of this pain. But God would not let me be overcome by it all. Through church, friends, and most of all Himself, I am making it. Each morning, sometimes through tears, I have asked God to give me the strength to be the kind of mother that I need to be.

It is so easy to become overwhelmed by the future and the questions that arise. Will we always need a baby-sitter? How will we pay for therapy? Can we have children who are not disabled? Yet I have found that God gives strength for today and provides miracles along the way to show me He is in control of this situation. I am reminded constantly that I cannot do it by myself and need to give God my weaknesses so that He can give me His strength. God continually reminds me that He created my son just the way he is (fearfully and wonderfully made), and that He loves my son despite all of his limitations.

I don't understand why this happened to us, and I live in a strange paradox of wanting my son to be "normal" and realizing that if he were normal, he wouldn't be the boy that I love so much now. I know that his disability will be a challenge for me for the rest of my life, but I also know that God is in control and provides me with His strength to get through each day. The storm that God has placed in my life is also one of the greatest gifts He has given me because it has taught me to rely on Him.

I really think I'm so different from others. My advice probably wouldn't set well with many. I have found humor in every phase of this [battle with cancer]. People's comments on my hairstyle make me laugh. Especially the lady who said she was tempted to shave her head and buy a wig, just so she could have hair like mine. (She didn't know mine was a wig.) When I look in the mirror, I think about how I've never been bald. Even when I was born I had a ton of hair. So now I know the shape of my head. I've looked at this as more of an adventure — waiting to see what the Lord is going to do through it — rather than a trial. That doesn't mean I want it, but it sure makes it easier to go through. When you think about it, really isn't it an honor that He chose to use me as a vessel for Him? There are so many others who are stronger and would have made a better witness, but He chose me. Pretty awesome, don't you think?

It was more like a "tornado" touching down, devastating madness, moving from one location to another in a little less than two years, four cancer-related surgeries, quintuple bypass, four months of chemotherapy. Barely recovered, I soon realized the Lord had more in store for me. In His wisdom He took to Himself, without warning or a chance to say good-bye, my best friend of fifty-five years. Suddenly my physical condition became irrelevant. Losing your spouse and knowing where she is, half of you is in heaven. But there is not a day I do not rejoice, knowing that our separation is very, very temporary.

Do I grieve? Sure, I do. Do I weep? Many times. Do I feel sorry for myself? Not with a caring Father at my side because, according to Psalm 66:19-20, He is faithful to His children: "God hath heard me; he hath attended to the voice of my prayer. Blessed be God, which hath not turned away my prayer nor his mercy from me." Can I ask for anything more? Our comfort comes from the Lord, and I think His loving heart hurts for us. His promises are true, and He will give you daily grace to walk this new road.

Suffering enabled me to experience blessings I never would have had otherwise. The little things in life were no longer taken for granted. Not knowing if our handicapped son would ever walk or talk made us celebrate every small achievement. We praised God for any milestone he passed, no matter how great or small. Our two older children developed normally and sailed through the typical milestones; we took them for granted. With Allen we celebrated his first little crawl, sitting up by himself, and finally at age three walking with a walker! Nothing was taken for granted. God was good, and we were receiving His blessings.

Our son was born eight weeks premature following a complicated pregnancy. At seven months old he started having daily seizures. The prognosis was poor, the possibility of mental retardation very high. He was also diagnosed with cerebral palsy. I never would have thought I could make it through such a traumatic experience. I remember the day my husband and I were sharing about all that was happening in our lives. I was so amazed to acknowledge that we were both coping well. God had indeed kept His promise to give me strength in all situations. I did not worry about our son's uncertain future but learned to rely on Christ's strength for today.

EMPLOYMENT

I was unemployed for three years. Whether you call it "laid off," "downsized," "position eliminated," or just plain "fired," losing a job has a dramatic impact on oneself, one's family, and neighbors.

Reaction varies from pity to condolences to empty offers of assistance to reactions similar to having a communicable disease.

It was easy early on to be self-absorbed, and it is probably a necessary part of the process. I wrongly grasped for the book of Job, trying to identify with him as mounting financial trials and sleepless nights continually surfaced. I say wrongly, because Job's predicament was incidental to the story, as was mine.

As my trial matured, I saw that my unemployment was merely a tool showing where my faith's strengths and weaknesses were. I realized that my strength and determination to solve this problem alone were misguided. I would not emerge whole unless I clung to Jesus Christ as a man cast adrift on the open seas clings to a life ring.

Finally it was obvious that James and other texts stressing service were more appropriate to my situation. Service doesn't eliminate financial concerns but re-instills a sense of purpose or identity that unemployment rips from us. Service re-instilled my sense of worth to the family of God. Service and God's Word enabled me to weather my storm of life.

GENERAL

As you know, God teaches us many, many things through our storms — even self-inflicted storms. Two lessons still stand out to me, now fourteen years after the storm. Both lessons bring benefits still today.

First, I know that the Holy Spirit will do things that seem totally impossible for me to accomplish. When we desire so much to make something happen, to bring a desired result or affect a needed change, we exhaust ourselves in trying to make it happen, especially when we desire to see comfort or rest in our spouse who may still be reeling from trauma or flashbacks. Learn to trust in the work of the Holy Spirit. He is able to do abundantly more. I now count on Him to work where no amount of human intervention can.

Second, when our best-laid plans and hard work and all we have envisioned and pursued with godly ambition seem to crumble before our eyes, we must rest in knowing that God's Plan B must be better than our Plan A. God knows us better than we know ourselves. He knows the future. We need to trust Him when He gives our journey a new direction. We need to be willing to cede our visions to His when the unforeseen occurs. Be willing to embrace His plan with faith-filled confidence.

Here are my thoughts regarding things learned while going through difficult times: 1) Satan will try to use unbiblical guilt to beat you up and hold you down. If you have truly confessed and repented of your sin, and your life shows the effects of the changing power of the Holy Spirit, then feelings of burdensome guilt that utterly weigh you down are not of Christ. Remember, as far as the east is from the west, that is how far Christ has removed our sins, and He remembers them no more. You may never escape the consequences of your sin, but the unrelenting guilt and "feeling bad" about your sin should not be part of your daily life.

2) Utter childlike faith is the only way to survive the storms of life. You must be brought to the point where you finally believe that you do *not* know best — God does. You must accept this fact and trust that He knows what He is doing, that He is completely sovereign and that He who began a good work in you *will* perfect it until the day of salvation. Trust — do not question God — believe that He is good.

INSPIRING QUOTATIONS

"Contrary to what might be expected, I look back on experiences that at the time seemed especially desolating and painful with particular satisfaction. Indeed, I can say with complete truthfulness that everything I have learned in my seventy-five years in this world, everything that has truly enhanced and enlightened my existence, has been through affliction and not through happiness, whether pursued or attained. In other words, if it ever were to be possible to eliminate affliction from our earthly existence by means of some drug or other medical mumbo jumbo, as Aldous Huxley envisaged in *Brave New World,* the result would not be to make life delectable, but to make it too banal and trivial to be endurable. This, of course, is what the Cross signifies. And it is the Cross, more than anything else, that has called me inexorably to Christ." (Malcolm Muggeridge)[1]

"There is no pit so deep that God's love is not deeper still." (Corrie Ten Boom)

GOD IN THE STORM

When God wants to drill a man,
And thrill a man,
And skill a man;
When God wants to mold a man
To play the noblest part,
When he yearns with all his heart
To create so great and bold a man
That all the world shall be amazed,
Watch his methods, watch his ways —

How he ruthlessly perfects
Whom he royally elects.
How he hammers him and hurts him,
And with mighty blows, converts him
Into trial shapes of clay
Which only God understands.

While his tortured heart is crying,
And he lifts beseeching hands.
How he bends but never breaks
When his good he undertakes.
How he uses
Whom he chooses,
And with every purposes, fuses him,
By every act, induces him
To try his splendor out.
God knows what he's about.

AUTHOR UNKNOWN

JESUS, LOVER OF MY SOUL

Jesus, lover of my soul, let me to Thy bosom fly,
While the nearer waters roll, while the tempest is high:
Hide me, O my Savior, hide, till the storm of life is past;
Safe into the haven guide, oh, receive my soul at last!

Other refuge have I none, hangs my helpless soul on Thee;
Leave, ah! leave me not alone, still support and comfort me!
All my trust on Thee is stayed, all my help from Thee I bring;
Cover my defenseless head with the shadow of Thy wing.

Thou, O Christ, art all I want; more than all in Thee I find:
Raise the fallen, cheer the faint, heal the sick, and lead the blind.
Just and holy is Thy name; I am all unrighteousness;
False and full of sin I am, Thou art full of truth and grace.

Plenteous grace with Thee is found, grace to cover all my sin;
Let the healing streams abound; make and keep me pure within:
Thou of life the fountain art, freely let me take of Thee;
Spring Thou up within my heart, rise to all eternity.

CHARLES WESLEY, 1740

NOTES

Chapter One: God of the Storms

1. *Modern Reformation*, September 2002, p. 46.
2. Ibid., p. 25.
3. Ibid., pp. 38-39.
4. John Piper, *The Misery of Job and the Mercy of God* (Wheaton, IL: Crossway Books, 2002), p. 9.

Chapter Two: God with Us

1. Quoted in Ken Gire, *The Weathering Grace of God* (Ann Arbor, MI: Servant, 2001), p 65.
2. Ibid., p. 52.
3. Quoted in *A Reason for Hope* (Wheaton, IL: Crossway Books, 2001), p. 42.

Chapter Three: God's Purposes for the Storms

1. Nancy Guthrie, *Holding on to Hope: A Pathway Through Suffering to the Heart of God* (Wheaton, IL: Tyndale House, 2004), p. 55.
2. C. S. Lewis, *The Problem of Pain* (San Francisco: HarperSanFrancisco, 2001).
3. John MacArthur, *Hebrews* (Chicago: Moody Press, 1983), p. 328.

Chapter Four: The God Who Provides

1. Scott J. Hafemann, *2 Corinthians* (Grand Rapids, MI: Zondervan, 2000), p. 463.

Appendix: Testimonies of Fellow Pilgrims

1. Malcolm Muggeridge, *A Twentieth Century Testimony* (Nashville: Thomas Nelson, 1978), quoted in Charles R. Swindoll, *Living on the Ragged Edge* (Nashville: Word, 1985), p. 71.